Oxford School *Shakespeare*

the Merchant of Venice

edited by
Roma Gill, OBE
M.A. *Cantab.*, B. Litt. *Oxon*

OXFORD
UNIVERSITY PRESS

OXFORD
UNIVERSITY PRESS

Great Clarendon Street, Oxford ox2 6dp

Oxford University Press is a department of the University of Oxford.
It furthers the University's objective of excellence in research, scholarship, and
education by publishing worldwide in
Oxford   New York

Auckland Cape Town Dar es Salaam Hong Kong Karachi
Kuala Lumpur Madrid Melbourne Mexico City Nairobi
New Delhi Shanghai Taipei Toronto

With offices in

Argentina Austria Brazil Chile Czech Republic France Greece
Guatemala Hungary Italy Japan Poland Portugal Singapore
South Korea Switzerland Thailand Turkey Ukraine Vietnam

© Oxford University Press 1979
Schools edition first published 1979
First revised edition published 1992
This second revised edition first published 2001
This third revised edition first published 2006
Trade edition first published 1994
This revised edition first published 2001

ISBN-10: 019 832152 x
ISBN-13: 978 019 832152 1

1 3 5 7 9 10 8 6 4 2

Illustrations by Alexy Pendle

All photographs by Donald Cooper (Photostage) with the exception of p. 110,
and the following: pXXV11 Capital Pictures; p113 Shakespeare's Globe;
p129 Corbis UK Ltd.

Cover image by Capital Pictures.

Oxford School Shakespeare
edited by Roma Gill, with additional material by Judith Kneen

Printed in Great Britain by Creative Print and Design Wales, Ebbw Vale.

Contents

Introduction

About the Play

A pound of flesh. You may know the expression, meaning 'the full and exact repayment of some debt or duty'. It's part of the English language, and the common property of people all over the world who have never heard of *The Merchant of Venice*. But this is where it began.

Money

The play is all about money – and as soon as you say that word, clichés come tumbling out. Money is not the most important thing in life, won't bring you happiness, can't buy me love, and is the root of all evil (a common misquotation[1]). For Portia, who has lots of it, wealth is almost an embarrassment and certainly an obstacle when it comes to finding a husband. For Shylock (who loses his daughter but complains more loudly about the ducats – Venetian gold coins – that she has stolen from him), money still means less than the opportunity to be revenged on his rival. And at the beginning of the play Antonio, a prince among Venetian merchants and a successful dealer in sumptuous luxury goods, is unspeakably and unaccountably depressed. Only Bassanio, broke and reckless, is reasonably cheerful: he has a plan, and just needs funding. His crazy idea – shoot another arrow in the direction of the one you've lost and you'll find both – triggers the action, and sets both of the play's main plots in motion.

Bassanio can be sure of a loan from his affectionate friend Antonio, but Antonio's money is all tied up in his business ventures, and so he turns to Shylock, a professional moneylender, who demands an unusual security for the loan – a pound of Antonio's flesh.

Shylock the Jew

Shylock is a Jew, a member of a race feared and despised by the Elizabethans for reasons that are complex and historical, and only partly religious. The Jews were hated for their biblical role in the

---

[1] 'for *the love of money* is the root of all evil', 1 Timothy 6:10.

crucifixion of Jesus and European countries from the twelfth century onwards had used this as a pretext for expelling them from their shores. Those who remained were often forbidden to own property, or to engage in any of the professions, and were thereby forced into the business of usury – lending money for profit. And mercantile societies need moneylenders. Some Jews prospered, and in England their success intensified the distrust of the native English, although Queen Elizabeth numbered a Jewish woman among her ladies-in-waiting, and even, for a time, had a Jewish doctor as her private physician – although Dr Lopez was eventually (in 1594) charged with trying to poison her, and executed.

All through the play we are aware of anti-Semitic prejudice in many of the characters, but Shakespeare himself takes no sides. His plot, based on a narrative fiction, demanded a Jewish villain – but Shakespeare understood human suffering and that Jews had for centuries been subject to humiliating discrimination, and he allows Shylock to speak for all persecuted minorities:

> Hath not a Jew eyes? Hath not a Jew hands, organs, dimensions, senses, affections, passions? Fed with the same food, hurt with the same weapons, subject to the same diseases, healed by the same means, warmed and cooled by the same winter and summer as a Christian is? If you prick us, do we not bleed?

If we can appreciate this argument, then it is hard not to agree with its logical extension –

> And if you wrong us, shall we not revenge?

Antonio is in serious danger when the underdog (Shylock) tries to seize his opportunity for triumph – but this is a comedy, and the good fairy comes to his rescue in the person of Portia, the first of Shakespeare's truly great female roles.

A woman's role

Most modern girls would find Portia's situation intolerable: a wealthy heiress, she has to obey the wishes of her dead father and agree to the test he has arranged to choose a husband for her – though not without showing a shadow of resentment that 'the will of a living daughter [should be] curbed by the will of a dead father'. She can only act, however, as every daughter of that time, never questioning a man's right to the ownership of all his wife's possessions, and resigning herself happily into the protection of Bassanio – who has won the lottery:

> But now, I was the lord
> Of this fair mansion, master of my servants,
> Queen o'er myself; and even now, but now,
> This house, these servants, and this same myself
> Are yours, my lord's.

Only for the past hundred years or so has a woman in England been allowed to keep her own property after marriage – and sexual discrimination is still felt and practised even today.

A modern tragedy

The *Merchant of Venice* deals with topics and social issues that belong as much, or even more, to the twenty-first century as they did to Shakespeare's own day – fathers and daughters, racial discrimination, colour prejudice, love and friendship. And to all of these there is some financial aspect. Altered attitudes in the twentieth century shifted the emphasis of Shakespeare's play so that it nearly became the *tragedy* of 'The Jew of Venice' (always an alternative title), but the magic of the final Act is powerful. The serious issues and complex figures of the trial scene dissolve into the moonlit serenity of Belmont, and laughter returns the characters and the audience to the real world with Gratiano's final bawdy joke.

Leading Characters in the Play

Antonio   The merchant of the play's title. He is a good and generous man, who promises to pay Shylock the money borrowed by Bassanio or else allow Shylock to cut off a pound of his flesh. His part in the play is rather a passive one, and he reveals his character mainly in his generosity to his friend and in his hatred of the Jew.

Bassanio   A young man who has already spent all his own money and now hopes to restore his fortunes by marrying an heiress. He needs to borrow money so that he can make a fine display when he courts Portia, and it is for his sake that Antonio enters into the bond with Shylock. Bassanio shows good judgement in his choice of caskets, and wins Portia for his wife.

Gratiano   A young man with a reputation for wild behaviour. He accompanies Bassanio to Belmont, and wins the love of Portia's lady-in-waiting, Nerissa.

Lorenzo   He is in love with Jessica, Shylock's daughter, and plans to steal her from her father's house.

Portia   The most important character in the play. She is an heiress, and is in love with Bassanio; but her father has devised a test involving three caskets, and Portia must marry the man who chooses the right casket. Portia is intelligent as well as beautiful; dressed as a lawyer she goes to Venice and saves Antonio from being killed by Shylock. Her home is Belmont, and the peace and harmony here contrast with the tense business world of Venice.

Nerissa   Portia's lady-in-waiting, who falls in love with Gratiano. When Portia goes to Venice as a lawyer, Nerissa accompanies her, dressed as a lawyer's clerk.

Shylock   A money lender, who is hated for his greed and because he is Jewish. He is Antonio's enemy, and when Bassanio's money is not repaid he demands the pound of flesh that Antonio promised as a forfeit.

Jessica Shylock's daughter; she disguises herself as a boy in order to run away from her father's house, where she is unhappy. She is in love with Lorenzo, a Christian.

Lancelot Gobbo The comedian of the play. He is at first Shylock's servant, then goes to work for Bassanio. His clowning often takes the form of misusing the English language; it is sometimes a welcome break from the tense or romantic scenes.

Synopsis

ACT 1

SCENE 1   Antonio is very depressed; he is willing to fund Bassanio's expedition to Belmont, but must try to borrow money from Shylock to do so.

SCENE 2   Portia longs to find a husband, but all her suitors must submit to a test arranged by her father before his death.

SCENE 3   Shylock agrees to lend money to Antonio – but he demands an unusual bond.

ACT 2

SCENE 1   Portia interviews a new suitor, the Prince of Morocco, and explains the terms of her father's will.

SCENE 2   Lancelot Gobbo wants to leave Shylock, his master, and find employment with Bassanio, who is preparing for his trip to Belmont.

SCENE 3   Lancelot says goodbye to Jessica, Shylock's daughter, who gives him a letter for Lorenzo, the Christian man she is in love with.

SCENE 4   Lorenzo is planning some late-night entertainment when Lancelot brings Jessica's letter.

SCENE 5   Shylock leaves Jessica in charge of his house.

SCENE 6   Lorenzo and his friends rescue Jessica from her father's house.

SCENE 7   The Prince of Morocco examines the caskets and makes his choice.

SCENE 8   Salarino and Solanio gossip about the news: Lorenzo and Jessica are missing, Shylock has been robbed, and Antonio is in trouble.

SCENE 9   Another suitor makes his choice – and Portia learns that Bassanio is coming to Belmont.

ACT 3

SCENE 1   Trouble for Antonio: Shylock rejoices in his power over the merchant –
and laments the loss of his daughter.

SCENE 2   Bassanio makes his choice of caskets, winning Portia for his wife.
Nerissa agrees to marry Gratiano, and both marriage contracts are
sealed with rings. Lorenzo and Jessica arrive in Belmont, bringing a
letter from Antonio.

SCENE 3   Antonio has been arrested and Shylock threatens him.

SCENE 4   Portia and Nerissa plan a visit to Venice.

SCENE 5   Lancelot teases Jessica.

ACT 4

SCENE 1   The trial. Antonio is prepared to die when Shylock refuses to show
mercy, but Portia, disguised as a young lawyer, tricks Shylock out of his
bond and asks Bassanio for his ring as a reward.

SCENE 2   Portia gets Bassanio's ring – and Nerissa plans to get her own from
Gratiano.

ACT 5

SCENE 1   Lorenzo teases Jessica as they wait in the moonlight. Portia and Nerissa
return from Venice, followed by Bassanio and Gratiano – who are
embarrassed when their wives demand to see the rings. All is explained,
and Portia has good news for Antonio.

The Merchant of Venice: Commentary

The action of the play takes place in Venice and in Belmont. Belmont is imaginary, but Venice is real. The city is located on the sea coast in the north of Italy, and is in fact built over a lagoon. Its main streets are canals, and the only vehicles are boats. In the sixteenth century, Venice was the centre for international trade, importing goods from all corners of the earth, and exporting them in the same way. We are told that Antonio, the greatest of the merchants, is waiting for his ships to return

> From Tripolis, from Mexico, and England,
> From Lisbon, Barbary, and India.   (3, 2, 266–7)

To be successful, a merchant had to invest his money wisely – and have luck on his side. Trading by sea was hazardous, and a sudden storm, or unseen rocks, could easily wreck a ship and drown the merchant's hopes along with the cargo.

ACT 1

SCENE 1   When his friends see that Antonio is depressed, they immediately think that he is worried about his ships at sea. They are sympathetic, and Solanio does his best to make light of the situation by exaggerating his fears to make his friend smile. But Antonio is sad for some other reason, and when we meet his dearest friend, Bassanio, we begin to guess at this reason. Bassanio is a carefree young man, who cheerfully admits that he has spent all of his own money and a good deal of Antonio's. However, Bassanio now has a scheme for increasing his wealth. Before he gives any details, he explains his theory: a lost arrow (he says) can often be found by shooting another arrow in the same direction, and watching carefully to see where it falls. The theory is, as Bassanio acknowledges, a 'childhood proof'; he believed it when he was a schoolboy, and now he wants to put it to the test again, spending more money in the hope of winning back what he has lost. This is not a very sensible, or responsible, way to act, but Bassanio emphasizes his youth and innocence. Perhaps he hopes that Antonio will treat him as though he were a child, and ignore the irresponsibility of his demand for more money to spend.

Bassanio next tells Antonio of an heiress, who has already given him some unspoken encouragement. Her name is Portia, and Bassanio claims to have fallen in love with her. He may be speaking the truth, but it is clear that the lady's wealth is a very attractive feature for him. Antonio promises to help him, but all the money he has is tied up in his own business ventures. Still, his 'credit' is good, and Bassanio can borrow all the ducats he needs to present himself to Portia as an eligible suitor, giving Antonio's name as security – that is, promising that Antonio will repay the debt if he himself is unable to do so.

Our feelings towards Bassanio at the end of this scene cannot be very warm, despite his youthful optimism. He has wasted a lot of money, both his own and his friend's. It seems that he wants to marry Portia not just for love, but also for her money. But he himself, perhaps unconsciously, shows what we should feel about him when he explains that his youth has been 'something too prodigal'. Repeated phrases throughout the play compare Bassanio with the Prodigal Son of Christ's parable (St Luke 15:11–32), who spent all his inheritance in 'riotous living'. When he was penniless and starving, he went repentantly back to his father's house, where he was welcomed with rejoicing. Bassanio has been 'prodigal'; now he asks for a chance to redeem himself.

Like the Prodigal Son's father, Antonio has shown the loving and forgiving generosity of his nature, but he remains a mysterious character. Early in the scene he tells Gratiano that he thinks of the world as 'A stage where every man must play a part, / And mine a sad one'. It is his changing relationship with Bassanio that causes his melancholy. Some Elizabethans thought – as the Greeks and Romans did – that the friendship between two men was a more spiritual bond, and should be more highly esteemed, than the love between a man and a woman. Knowing that Bassanio is interested in a lady (see lines 119–21), Antonio may be secretly grieving for the inevitable end to a friendship.

SCENE 2   From the hearty, but anxious, masculine world of Venice, we move to the feminine peace of Belmont. Even here there is anxiety, as Portia's opening sigh indicates. It is now Nerissa who tries to cheer Portia, but she cannot take her mistress's mind off the situation where she is surrounded by suitors and yet 'cannot choose one, nor refuse none'. Shakespeare has to communicate to his audience a lot of information about the test that Portia's father devised for the men who wish to marry her. The information is given gradually, in five separate scenes, so that we seem to discover the facts just as the suitors do. For the moment, we are just told that each candidate must make a choice between three caskets.

Nerissa explains why Portia must obey this somewhat ridiculous order when she says that 'holy men at their death have good inspirations'. Proverbially, at this time, it was believed that a good man would be divinely inspired, and might even speak prophetically, when he was close to death. To disobey or disregard such a prophecy was considered almost sacrilege.

The two young women amuse themselves by gossiping about the suitors who have already assembled at Belmont. Although Portia and Nerissa are Italian, they share a sense of humour which is undoubtedly English. As they laugh about each man's peculiarities, we can learn something of what the Elizabethans thought of their continental neighbours — and also of how they could laugh at themselves. The 'young baron of England' is a caricature of the Englishman abroad, in the twenty-first century as well as in the sixteenth: the English have never been good at speaking foreign languages! Nor is there a 'national dress' for England, such as many other countries possess; the English were always content (it seems) to imitate the costumes of other countries. The joke about the Scottish lord would have a topical significance for Shakespeare's audience. At this time England and Scotland were separate kingdoms, and in their frequent quarrels the French always promised to aid the Scots (but rarely kept their promises).

We are never allowed to see this 'parcel of wooers', for Nerissa tells Portia that they have all decided to return home, not trying their luck with the caskets. There is no doubt that Portia is glad they are leaving. Nerissa reminds her of a young Venetian whom Portia met whilst her father was alive, and the speed with which Portia recalls Bassanio's name is enough to tell us that she remembers him with pleasure. Bassanio is described by Nerissa as 'a scholar and a soldier'. These qualities made up the ideal courtier in Elizabethan eyes, and the description may help to prepare us for a Bassanio who is rather different from the one we left in Venice.

Portia's enthusiasm dies away, and her weary resignation returns, when she is told that a new suitor is approaching Belmont. It is the Prince of Morocco, and the title arouses her prejudice as she goes inside to prepare for his arrival.

SCENE 3   Meanwhile, in Venice, Bassanio has found a usurer who can lend the money he needs. Shylock is very cautious, repeating each of Bassanio's demands to make sure that they are perfectly understood. His deliberation makes Bassanio nervous, and he shows irritation when Shylock says that 'Antonio is a good man'. The word 'good' has different implications: Bassanio thinks that it refers to Antonio's character, and he is angry that such a man as Shylock should presume to judge his friend. Shylock, having succeeded in annoying Bassanio, hastens to explain that by 'good' he meant only 'sufficient' – financially sound. The two disagree again over the interpretation of 'assur'd', by which Bassanio means that Shylock may trust Antonio; Shylock says that he will indeed be 'assur'd', meaning that he will take all precautions to protect himself and his money.

Bassanio's polite invitation to dinner is refused by Shylock in words that introduce the theme of racial hatred: he thinks he would be asked 'to smell pork', a meat forbidden to Jews by their religion. Shylock perhaps speaks these words '*aside*', not talking directly to Bassanio but uttering his thoughts aloud for the audience alone to hear them, just as only the audience hears the soliloquy in which Shylock reveals his attitude to Antonio. Religious feeling has some part to play in this attitude, but a minor one compared with the hostility he bears towards a business rival.

We learn that Antonio disapproves morally of lending money for interest (and it is a mark of his affection for Bassanio that he is prepared now to break his own rules). Shylock justifies his activities by telling the story of Jacob from the Old Testament (Genesis 30:31–43). Jacob was angry with Laban, his uncle, and tried to outwit him, using his skill as a shepherd. He believed that the ewes, seeing the striped twigs in front of them when they conceived, would give birth to striped or spotted lambs, which Laban had agreed should become Jacob's wages. This indeed happened, but whereas Shylock applauds Jacob's cunning, Antonio (and most devout Jews) ascribed the success to the hand of God.

The merchant and the usurer engage in passionate argument. Shylock reveals the cruel insults he has had to suffer from Antonio in the past, but Antonio stands firm in his contempt for the Jew. He refuses to borrow the money as a friend, but urges Shylock, with words that he will regret, to

> lend it rather to thine enemy,
> Who if he break, thou may'st with better face
> Exact the penalty.

Shylock proposes 'a merry sport' which Antonio, surprisingly, is willing to accept. He agrees to the forfeit that Shylock suggests – 'an equal pound of your fair flesh' – to be given if the money cannot be properly repaid.

The words 'kind' and 'kindness' are repeated several times at the end
of this scene. They have a surface meaning – 'generous' and 'generosity'
– which Antonio accepts, and an ironic double meaning. If Shylock
'grows kind' in this second sense, he will become even more like
himself, true to his nature. And we have already, in his soliloquy, seen
what this is.

ACT 2

SCENE 1   Prejudice is the subject of the short episode in Belmont, where we see
Portia's reception of the Prince of Morocco. The prince's appearance
shows that he is an exotic figure: the stage direction, probably written
by Shakespeare himself, describes him as 'a tawny [brown] Moor, all in
white'. His first speech reinforces our sense that he is excitingly different
from the Europeans that we have seen so far, but it does not change
Portia's mind. She is polite, but we understand, better than Morocco
can, what she means when she tells him that, in her eyes, he is 'as fair /
As any comer I have look'd on yet'. We have heard what Portia thought
of her other suitors. The Prince's reply to this ambiguous remark does
not encourage our good opinion of him. He boasts of his own courage
and achievements in a very exaggerated language, and so loses some of
our sympathy.

We are given a new piece of information concerning the casket test.
The men who choose wrongly must never again think of marrying. It is
now clear why the earlier suitors left Belmont without trying their luck;
Morocco, however, is not deterred, and prepares to make his choice.

Whilst Morocco is taking his oath in the 'temple' – many great
houses at this time had their own private chapels – Shakespeare returns
us to Venice. The next five scenes will bring Bassanio from Venice to
Belmont, and develop the romance of the plot through the
introduction of Jessica, Shylock's daughter. But first, Shakespeare must
create a role for the leading comic actor in his dramatic company – the
part of Lancelot Gobbo, Shylock's servant.

SCENE 2   Comedy scenes such as this are the most difficult and unrewarding to
read; they need to be performed, so that the actor can introduce the
visual effects that the lines demand. When Lancelot pretends to be torn
between his conscience and the devil, he might (for instance) jump to
the left when the devil is speaking – because devils traditionally
appeared on the left – and to the right when 'conscience' replies. There
could be humour in the difference between Lancelot's appearance (as
the miserly Shylock's servant he would not be well dressed) and his

grand manner of speech to the old man; this would emphasize the comedy of the 'mistaken identity' situation. When Old Gobbo feels his son's head and comments on his 'beard', it is obvious from Lancelot's reply that he has got hold of the hair tied at the back of his neck; and if Lancelot passes his father's hand across his fingers, implying that they are his ribs ('You may tell every finger I have with my ribs'), the comedy will increase with the old man's confusion.

The English language is a very complicated one, and even English people make mistakes when they speak it. There are many words that sound grand – but sometimes those who use them do not understand their meanings, or else confuse one word with another that sounds similar. This is especially likely to happen when the speakers are trying to create a good impression of themselves. Lancelot and his father are doing this when they address Bassanio. They are conscious that Bassanio is a gentleman, whilst they are only peasants, and they try to use what they think is the proper language of gentlemen. Even in the twenty-first century, when class distinctions are much less clearly marked than they were in the sixteenth, the writers of television comedy still find subjects for laughter in our linguistic snobbishness. Lorenzo's comment is valid today: 'How every fool can play upon the word' (Act 3, Scene 5, line 38).

Bassanio is in a good temper, and responds well to Lancelot's fooling; he agrees to employ him and give him 'a livery / More guarded than his fellows'. A 'guarded' uniform – one decorated with yellow braid – was often worn by the professional fool in a gentleman's household; perhaps this is the function that Bassanio intends for Lancelot when he becomes 'The follower of so poor a gentleman'.

Even though he admits he is poor, Bassanio is already behaving with his former extravagance now that he has got Shylock's money. He is planning to give a party before he leaves Venice. However, he shows a more sedate side of his character when Gratiano asks to accompany him to Belmont. Gratiano turns Bassanio's solemn warning into comedy. He promises to behave in a way that is very sober, but at the same time quite ridiculous, and he probably accompanies his speech with exaggerated gestures.

SCENE 3 When Jessica gives Lancelot the letter for Lorenzo, the short scene takes the plot a stride further – and also serves to increase our dislike for Shylock. We learn that his 'house is hell', and that Jessica is 'asham'd to be [her] father's child', although she recognizes that it is a 'heinous sin' for a daughter to have such feelings.

SCENE 4   The letter is delivered to Lorenzo as he and his friends are discussing their costumes for Bassanio's party. It was quite usual, in Shakespeare's time, for a small band of the guests at a grand feast to disguise themselves in elaborate costumes and entertain the other guests with a masque – a performance with singing and dancing. Page-boys carried torches for the masquers, and Lorenzo suddenly realizes how he can steal Jessica away from her father's house: she can be disguised as his page.

SCENE 5   There can scarcely be a greater contrast than that between the lively young men planning their evening's entertainment, and the surly Shylock. He takes no pleasure in the feast, but has decided to 'go in hate, to feed upon / The prodigal Christian' (yet another comparison of Bassanio with the Prodigal Son). Shylock is determined to do all he can to ruin Bassanio, and he even considers that Lancelot's change of employer might 'help to waste / His borrow'd purse'.

SCENE 6   Gratiano's reference to the 'penthouse' under which they are standing is one of many remarks in Elizabethan drama that help us to reconstruct, in imagination, the kind of stage that Shakespeare was writing for. It seems that there was always a balcony, which allowed 'split-level' acting. In this scene the young men assemble on the main stage, underneath the 'penthouse' formed by the balcony on which Jessica appears, dressed as a boy. She is shy, because in Elizabethan times women *never* wore men's clothes. Her embarrassment is expressed with great delicacy, and it is easy to forget that Shakespeare and his contemporaries would probably have been a little amused by the situation. In many plays of this period the female characters put on masculine clothing, and a gentle comedy arises out of the fact that female characters were always played by boy actors: the boys dress up as girls, and then the 'girls' turn into boys.

Waiting for Jessica has made the masquers late for the feast, and now Antonio comes in search of Gratiano. The wind has changed, and it is time to set sail for Belmont.

SCENE 7   Whilst all the activity of Jessica's elopement has been taking place in Venice, the Prince of Morocco at Belmont has dined, and sworn an oath never to look for a wife if he fails the casket test. At last we see the caskets that we have heard so much about. Each one bears an inscription, which Morocco reads aloud. The gold and silver caskets make promises, but the leaden one is menacing. Morocco refuses to be threatened, and passes to the silver casket, which assures him that he 'shall get as much as he deserves'. We heard in Act 2, Scene 1 that he has a good opinion of himself, and he is naturally tempted to choose silver. The golden casket, however, offers 'what many men desire', and Morocco decides that this refers to Portia, because 'all the world desires her'. It would be an insult to Portia (he concludes) to associate her with lead, or even with silver; so he opens the golden casket.

The casket contains a skull, the emblem of death – which indeed many unhappy men do desire. Shocked and saddened, the Prince of Morocco departs immediately.

SCENE 8   In Venice, Shylock has discovered that his daughter is missing – and she has taken a lot of his money with her. Solanio gives a comical account of the Jew's confusion, when Shylock apparently did not know which loss to lament more. It is important that we do not *see* Shylock here, because his distress might create too much sympathy for him. Instead, we join Salarino and Solanio in their laughter.

But not everything in this scene is comic: there is bad news for Antonio. A ship has been wrecked in the English Channel, and it may well be his. The conversation becomes sober, as the two friends think of Antonio's generosity – 'A kinder gentleman treads not the earth' – and remind us of his great affection for Bassanio: 'I think he only loves the world for him'.

SCENE 9   Yet another suitor, the Prince of Arragon, has arrived at Belmont; he repeats the three promises that he has sworn to keep, and goes to make his choice of the three caskets. Like the Prince of Morocco, he reads the inscriptions, and speaks his thoughts aloud. The Prince of Arragon is excessively conscious of his social position, and insists that he is different from other men: he will not 'jump with common spirits', and look in the golden casket for 'what many men desire'. He is attracted by the promise of the silver casket: 'Who chooseth me shall get as much as he deserves'. For a time he meditates on the subject of nobility and merit, deploring the fact that 'low peasantry' (people of humble birth) can be found among noblemen – 'the true seed of honour'. Having convinced *himself* that he deserves to win Portia, he opens the silver casket. We are not surprised that this is the wrong choice, for Arragon has convinced *us* that he is far too conceited – although perhaps he deserves something better than 'the portrait of a blinking idiot'.

As soon as the Prince of Arragon has left, news is brought that another suitor is approaching. He has already made a good impression on Portia's servants with the 'Gifts of rich value' that he has sent to announce his coming; and we recognize the extravagance that is characteristic of Bassanio. Portia and Nerissa are hopeful.

ACT 3

SCENE 1   The optimism of Belmont gives place to the darkening atmosphere of Venice. There is still no confirmation that the ship wrecked in the English Channel is indeed Antonio's, but Solanio believes the rumour to be true. Shylock also has heard the report, and his anger over his daughter's flight is forgotten for a moment as he voices his hatred and resentment of Antonio. He has had to suppress his feelings for years, but now they explode violently. His passion increases, and so too does the sympathy of the audience. He appeals to common humanity: 'Hath not a Jew eyes? hath not a Jew hands . . . If you poison us, do we not die?' He becomes almost a hero, and certainly a human being – then suddenly he changes back into a monster: 'And if you wrong us, shall we not revenge?'

Salarino and Solanio are fortunately saved from having to reply to this tirade; they leave Shylock with another Jew, Tubal, who has news of Jessica.

Shylock experiences another confusion of emotions as Tubal imparts various pieces of information in an incoherent manner. Jessica is spending her father's money recklessly, and in exchange for a pet monkey she has given away the ring that was a token of betrothal from her mother to her father. Grief and anger conflict with malicious glee when Shylock hears of Antonio's misfortunes, and it is clear that he will take revenge for the loss of his daughter and his ring when he claims the forfeit from Antonio.

SCENE 2   Portia is happy in Bassanio's company, and she tries to persuade him to stay at Belmont for a few days before making his choice of the caskets. Her happiness is mingled with modesty, as she is too shy to tell Bassanio that she loves him. Bassanio too has fallen in love, but he cannot endure the uncertainty and feels that he must try his luck as soon as possible. Nerissa and the servants stand aside, leaving Portia and Bassanio almost alone on the stage. Music plays, while Portia watches the man she loves as he tries to make the decision that will bring happiness to both of them.

The song that helps to create a magic atmosphere also introduces Bassanio's meditation on appearance and reality. He is speaking only to himself – Portia does not hear him (just as he did not hear her words before the song). The audience, of course, knows which casket Bassanio must choose, because Shakespeare has already shown us the contents of the gold and silver caskets.

Portia is almost overcome with delight when Bassanio selects the 'meagre lead'; and when Bassanio finds 'Fair Portia's counterfeit' in the casket he is ecstatically happy. He praises the picture rapturously, and for a time cannot believe his luck.

A rather more materialistic note is heard in the metaphorical language when Portia wishes to 'stand high in [Bassanio's] *account*', and offers him 'the full *sum*' of herself; it is repeated when Gratiano refers to the '*bargain*' of their faith. But to balance this there is the ritual moment when Portia gives away all that she owns (including 'this same myself') and as a token places a ring on Bassanio's finger. Bassanio accepts the token, and binds himself to Portia:

> when this ring
> Parts from this finger, then parts life from hence.

Gratiano and Nerissa announce their intention of imitating Bassanio and Portia; and the happiness of the moment is complete.

It is now time to change the direction of the scene, and Shakespeare switches the mood with a bawdy joke (in prose).

The arrival of Salerio, Lorenzo, and Jessica is a welcome surprise, but the letter that Salerio has brought from Venice 'steals the colour from Bassanio's cheek'. Things have gone very badly for Antonio: he is ruined. Salerio tells of Shylock's eagerness to claim his bond from Antonio, and Jessica is able to bear witness to her father's fiendish malice: 'he would rather have Antonio's flesh / Than twenty times the value of the sum / That he did owe him'. Portia is more than able to pay back the three thousand ducats, but we can take no comfort from her offer. The situation seems hopeless, and when Antonio's pathetic letter is read aloud it destroys the last remaining scrap of the happiness established in the scene.

SCENE 3   A short scene shows us what the letter described. Antonio, in the custody of a jailer, meets Shylock. The Jew will hear no pleas for mercy, and Antonio knows that it is useless to speak to him. Solanio hopes that the Duke will be able to intervene in the dispute, but Antonio knows the importance of strict justice in the mercantile world of which Venice is the head. This is a subject that will be mentioned at Antonio's trial.

SCENE 4   Lorenzo has been telling Portia about Antonio, and Portia has decided that she and Nerissa will go away for a few days, leaving Belmont in the care of Lorenzo. She sends a servant to her cousin in Padua, asking for some 'notes and garments'. We understand the request for clothes when Portia explains to Nerissa that they are going to dress up as men, and that she herself will imitate all the mannerisms of a brash young man – including the voice that is 'between the change of man and boy'.

SCENE 5   The next scene, still at Belmont, does nothing to develop any plot. But it encourages the audience to imagine that enough time has passed to allow Portia and Nerissa to travel from Belmont to Venice; on a practical level, it gives the actors time to change from their female dresses to the male costumes required in the following scene. In addition, it provides an opportunity for the comedian to deliver some more of his word-play jokes in the part of Lancelot Gobbo – who of course accompanied his new master when Bassanio came to Belmont.

ACT 4

SCENE 1   The trial scene in *The Merchant of Venice* is one of the most famous scenes in English drama. It has given a phrase to the English language: people who have never heard of the play understand what it means to want one's 'pound of flesh'.

The conversation between the Duke and Antonio, before Shylock comes on to the stage, shows the hopeless resignation with which Antonio faces Shylock's wrath. The Duke makes a further plea for mercy, but Shylock is unmoved. He will admit that his hatred for Antonio is irrational and emotional: just as some people hate cats, or the sound of bagpipes, so (he says)

> can I give no reason, nor I will not,
> More than a lodg'd hate and a certain loathing
> I bear Antonio.

Antonio is not intimidated, and shows his contempt for Shylock's 'Jewish heart'. Bassanio offers to repay twice the money that he borrowed, but Shylock will not yield, and reminds the court that the pound of flesh is his by law. If the Duke refuses to grant this, it will appear that 'There is no force in the decrees of Venice'. We remember Antonio's words (Act 3, Scene 3, lines 26–31), and realize that, if the law is not observed, Venice will suffer in its reputation as the centre of international trade.

The Duke has made a final attempt to save Antonio legally. He has asked for the opinion of a famous lawyer, Bellario, and the court waits to hear this man's judgment. Bassanio is optimistic, but the tension of the situation has made Antonio even more resigned to his fate; he almost feels that he deserves to die.

The lawyer's clerk has brought a letter from Bellario, and whilst the Duke reads the letter, Shylock sharpens his knife. Gratiano cannot bear to see this sight, and he begins to abuse Shylock. The Jew appears to be unaffected by his insults, for he knows the strength of his position: 'I stand here for law'.

Bellario is sick, and cannot come to Venice; instead he has sent a legal colleague, 'a young doctor of Rome', who is fully acquainted with the case. The audience recognizes this 'doctor': it is Portia, and her 'clerk' is Nerissa – but, needless to say, the other characters of the play cannot see through the disguise.

Portia upholds Venetian law, but she urges Shylock to show mercy. She describes the 'quality of mercy' as a divine blessing, which benefits both the man who shows mercy and the man who receives it. The petition in the Lord's Prayer, 'forgive us our trespasses', comes to mind when Portia explains how mercy belongs to God; if this were not so, the whole human race would be damned for its sins. But this is Christian doctrine, and Shylock's religion is that of the Old Testament, which emphasizes the importance of the law, just as Shylock does now: 'I crave the law'.

Once again Bassanio offers the money; again Shylock refuses it; and once more we are reminded that a general principle lies beneath this particular instance: any deviation would be

> recorded for a precedent,
> And many an error by the same example
> Will rush into the state.

The statement is harsh, but it is correct. Portia has earned Shylock's praise: 'A Daniel come to judgement'. Daniel was 'a young youth', according to the 'Story of Susannah' in the *Apocrypha*. He was inspired by God to give judgement when the chaste Susannah was accused of adultery by two lascivious 'elders' who had tried to rape her.

Portia continues to win Shylock's approval as she instructs the court about the penalty that Antonio must pay. The knife is sharpened, and the scales are ready; Antonio prepares for death. He speaks a few words of comfort to Bassanio, ending with a wry jest about the debt:

> For if the Jew do cut but deep enough
> I'll pay it instantly with all my heart.

The tension is broken, but only for a moment, when Bassanio and Gratiano refer to their wives. The 'lawyer' and his 'clerk' are amused.

Just when Shylock is ready to cut into Antonio's flesh, Portia stops the proceedings. She reveals to Shylock the single flaw in his carefully worded bond: he is entitled to his pound of flesh, but has made no provision for a single drop of blood.

Gratiano exults over Shylock, repeating ironically all the words of praise that the Jew bestowed on the 'learned judge', and agreeing that he is indeed 'A second Daniel'. Like Portia, Daniel was not expected in the court, and the verdict he gave saved Susannah and condemned her accusers. The comparison is more apt now than it was when Shylock introduced it.

Shylock realizes that he cannot have his pound of flesh, and he tries to take the money that Bassanio is still offering. Now it is Portia's turn to be inflexible, and she insists that Shylock can have 'merely justice, and his bond'. When Shylock proposes to leave the court, Portia calls him back. The law of Venice has a strict penalty that must be paid by any 'alien' – foreigner – who tries to murder a Venetian. Shylock has thus offended, and for this crime his possessions are confiscated and his life is in danger. Antonio, of course, shows his generosity. Half of Shylock's wealth is forfeited to him, but he is willing to renounce his personal share and take the money on loan, keeping it in trust for Lorenzo, 'the gentleman / That lately stole his daughter'. He makes two conditions: firstly, Shylock must become a Christian; and, secondly, he must make a will leaving all that he possesses to Jessica and Lorenzo. Shylock is utterly defeated. He asks for permission to leave the court, and indicates his agreement to Antonio's conditions: 'send the deed after me / And I will sign it'.

It is now the function of Gratiano to swing the mood of the scene and the audience from near-tragedy to an almost light-hearted acceptance of the situation: this is only a play, and we are in England, where twelve 'godfathers' would make a jury.

It is only necessary now to pay the 'lawyer', and then Bassanio can take Antonio home to Belmont, to meet his new wife. The 'lawyer' refuses payment, then suddenly catches sight of a ring on Bassanio's finger, and requests this as a keepsake. It is the ring that Portia gave to Bassanio, telling him that if he should ever part with it for any reason, it would 'presage the ruin of [his] love'. Remembering this, Bassanio refuses; the 'lawyer' departs, apparently angry. Antonio begs Bassanio not to withhold the ring, and Bassanio cannot refuse the friend who risked so much for him.

Scene 2   Gratiano hurries after Portia to give her Bassanio's ring. Nerissa, still disguised as the lawyer's clerk, whispers to Portia that she will use a similar trick to get her own ring from Gratiano. The two girls laugh in anticipation of their husbands' embarrassment when they return to Belmont.

ACT 5

Scene 1   Moonlight and music emphasize the tranquillity of Belmont and its contrast with the harsh legal world of Venice. Lorenzo and Jessica are relaxed here, and Jessica's escape from the 'hell' of her father's house seems to be almost as remote in time as the mythological lovers who are recalled by the moonlight. The mood of the scene is saved from being over-romantic when the couple start to tease each other, and when the messengers break in with their news. Harmony is restored, however, when Lorenzo and Jessica are alone again. Lorenzo starts to explain the theory of the music of the spheres, made by the planets in their constant motion but beyond the hearing of human ears, which are deafened by the noises of earthly life.

     Portia's musicians appear, probably on the balcony, to 'draw [their mistress] home with music'. The beauty of Lorenzo's speech (when he describes the 'patens of bright gold', and the 'young-eyed cherubins') blends with the playing of the musicians to recreate, in human terms, the heavenly harmony. Lorenzo and Jessica fall silent; perhaps they are asleep.

Portia and Nerissa come from the opposite side of the stage as they approach Belmont from Venice. Their chatter breaks into the music, and the dream world becomes real. A trumpet announces the arrival of Bassanio, just as day is breaking. The missing rings provide a final gentle comedy, as the two embarrassed husbands try to justify their actions to wives who are trying to hide their amusement.

In the end, of course, all is happiness. Lorenzo and Jessica join the other two couples, and Portia gives Antonio a last surprise – the news that three of his ships 'Are richly come to harbour suddenly'. There can be no reaction from the audience other than Antonio's 'I am dumb', and final applause for Shakespeare. He has taken three main strands – the casket story, the bond story, and the ring story – and woven them into a single plot, which brings all three stories to a successful conclusion, and ensures that all the characters (with one exception) 'live happily ever after' – just as fairy-tale characters ought to do.

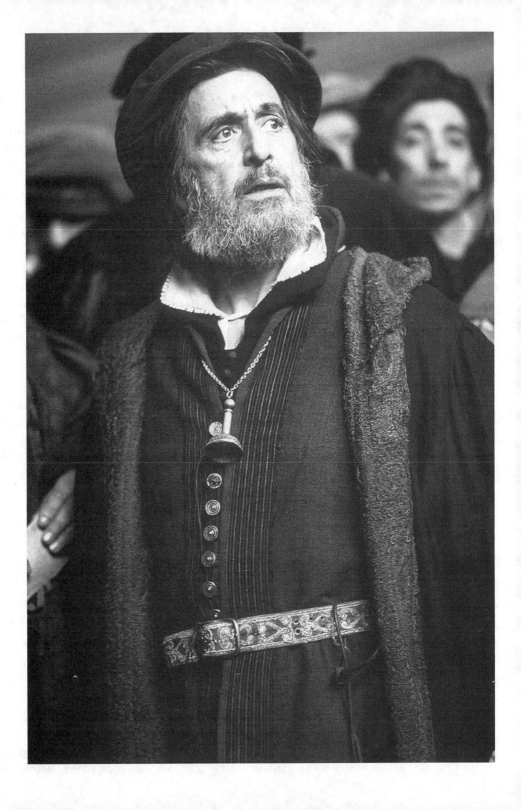

Shylock

A happy ending for the leading characters is essential for a romantic comedy such as *The Merchant of Venice*. But one very important character is left out of the general rejoicing in Act 5. Shylock has been defeated of his bond, robbed of his ducats, and deserted by his daughter; he is even compelled to give up his birthright, his Jewish religion, and become one of the Christians whom he so much hates. Does he deserve this fate? Is *The Merchant of Venice* a comedy for all the other characters, but a tragedy for Shylock?

Shakespeare took the story of Shylock's bond from an Italian novel, but the money-lending Jew in this source has no personality, and no daughter. Consequently we can assume that Shylock is Shakespeare's own creation: all the personality traits that we find in him were deliberately worked out by the dramatist, and not borrowed accidentally along with the plot.

Shylock the Jewish moneylender

Shylock starts from a double disadvantage, as far as an Elizabethan audience was concerned. He is a Jew, and he is a moneylender. There were not many Jews in England in the Middle Ages, but English Christians hated them, and this feeling was still strong in the sixteenth century. The Elizabethans also hated the traditional Jewish profession of usury – the lending of money for profit. Jews were often forbidden to own land or to engage in trade in England; consequently the only lucrative profession open to them was money lending. The Christians deplored this – in theory. In practice, the expanding economy of the times demanded that money should be readily available. Francis Bacon, who was Lord Chancellor of England in 1618, claimed that

> to speak of the abolishing of usury is idle. All states have ever had it, in one kind, or rate, or other. So as that opinion must be sent to Utopia. (Essay 'Of Usury')

Certainly, the usurer is necessary to the world of *The Merchant of Venice*. Shylock's wealth is evidence of his professional success, which could only come from satisfying a social need.

Shylock first appears as a cautious businessman, thinking carefully before he invests his three thousand ducats in Bassanio's enterprise. His reaction to the polite invitation to dinner is unexpected in its venom, which increases as he tells the audience of his hatred for Antonio.

Religious differences seem to be less important than professional jealousy:

> I hate him for he is a Christian;
> But more for that in low simplicity
> He lends out money gratis.

To some extent Shylock justifies his hostility when he describes how he has been treated by Antonio – insulted, spat upon, and kicked out of the way like 'a stranger cur'. Because of this, we sympathize with him. When the scene ends, we are left with two conflicting opinions of Shylock and his 'merry sport'. Are we to share Antonio's surprise, 'And say there is much kindness in the Jew'? Or is Bassanio right to be suspicious of 'fair terms and a villain's mind'?

Shylock the father

The scene with Antonio and Bassanio shows Shylock in his professional, public, life. Next, we hear what he is like at home. His comic servant, Lancelot Gobbo, exaggerates (with a characteristic misuse of the English language) when he says that 'the Jew is the very devil incarnation'. But this opinion is echoed by Shylock's daughter, Jessica, when she sighs 'Our house is hell'. Jessica is 'asham'd to be [her] father's child', although she knows that it is a 'heinous sin' for a daughter to have such feelings. We can understand Jessica's misery when her father gives instructions about locking up his house whilst he is away. Jessica is forbidden even to look out of the window to watch the masquers going to Bassanio's feast. Shylock is a killjoy – and he has also killed his daughter's natural affection for him.

Shakespeare does not let us see Shylock in his first frenzy of distress when he finds that Jessica is missing, because this would surely arouse our sympathy. Instead, Solanio describes the scene, and the audience is encouraged to share in his laughter. From Solanio's account, it seems that Shylock's grief over the loss of his daughter is equalled (perhaps even surpassed) by his anger at the theft of his money. He utters 'a passion so confus'd':

> My daughter! O my ducats! O my daughter!
> Fled with a Christian! O my Christian ducats!

Shylock the victim

When Shylock next appears (Act 3, Scene 1) the passion is subdued into an intense and malevolent bitterness; yet the jesting of the two Christians is cruel. The loss of a daughter is a real cause for sorrow, and

Shylock earns some pity (from the audience) when he tells Solanio and Salarino that 'my daughter is my flesh and my blood'.

It is with very mixed feelings, then, that we are led up to the powerful speech in which Shylock catalogues the abuses he has had to suffer from Christians in general, and from Antonio in particular. There is only one reason that he can see for this treatment: 'I am a Jew'. It is easy to respond to the rhetorical questions that follow:

> Hath not a Jew eyes? Hath not a Jew hands, organs, dimensions, senses, affections, passions? Fed with the same food, hurt with the same weapons, subject to the same diseases, healed by the same means, warmed and cooled by the same winter and summer, as a Christian is? If you prick us, do we not bleed? If you tickle us, do we not laugh? If you poison us, do we not die?

Shylock appeals to our common humanity. To give a negative answer to his questions would deny not *his* humanity, but our own. The speech, however, continues:

> and if you wrong us, shall we not revenge? If we are like you in the rest, we will resemble you in that . . . The villainy you teach me I will execute, and it shall go hard but I will better the instruction.

Common humanity ignores all limitations of colour, race, or creed; and this is strongly asserted in the first part of Shylock's speech. But the assertions of these last lines show that the individual – Shylock – is determined to ignore the limits of humanity. He will 'better the instruction', and prove himself to be not the *equal* of the Christians in inflicting suffering on others, but their *superior*.

Shylock's downfall

The events that follow do nothing to moderate the presentation of Shylock in the terms used by the Duke when he warns Antonio, before the trial begins, that his adversary is

> an inhuman wretch
> Uncapable of pity, void and empty
> From any dram of mercy.

During the trial, Shylock loses the audience's sympathy, by his words and by the action of sharpening the knife on the sole of his shoe (which Gratiano observes in Act 4, Scene 1, line 123). Neither insults nor pleading spoil the enjoyment of his triumph, and when sentence is given against Antonio, he repeats the words of the bond with a lingering relish:

> Ay, his breast.
> So says the bond, doth it not, noble judge?
> 'Nearest his heart': those are the very words.

Shylock demanded a strict observance of the law, and (in poetic justice) it is precisely this that defeats him. Gratiano exults over his downfall, but the other characters in the court speak no unnecessary words and show no satisfaction until Shylock has left the court. Even then, conversation is formal, occupied only with thanks and payment. It does not obliterate the memory of Shylock's parting words:

> I pray you give me leave to go from hence;
> I am not well.

A snarl of frustrated wrath can deliver this line; or else it can be spoken with the anguish of a man who has lost everything – his daughter, his wealth, his religious freedom, and the engagement ring given to him by his wife.

Shakespeare's Shylock

Recent English productions of *The Merchant of Venice* have emphasized the suffering human being, but I do not think that this is what Shakespeare intended. Shylock is more complex than any of the other characters in the play: we can think of him as a 'real' person, whose words and deeds are motivated by thoughts and feelings that we can discover from the play, and that we can understand when we have discovered them. We cannot think of Bassanio (for instance) in this way. Yet in admiring Shakespeare's achievement in the creation of Shylock, we must beware of danger. Often, when we know a person well, and understand why he acts as he does, we become sympathetic to him; in *The Merchant of Venice* we are further encouraged to sympathize with Shylock by the fact that other leading characters (such as Bassanio) do *not* compel our sympathies. Sympathy can give rise to affection, and affection often tempts us to withhold moral judgement, or at least be gentle in our censure. Shylock's conduct merits condemnation. We can only refrain from condemning it because we know that he has suffered for being a Jew; and this, surely, is another form of prejudice?

Shakespeare's Verse

Blank verse

Easily the best way to understand and appreciate Shakespeare's verse is to read it aloud – and don't worry if you can't understand everything! Try not to be influenced by the dominant rhythm, but decide which are the most important words in each line and use the regular metre to drive them forward to the listeners.

Shakespeare's plays are mainly written in 'blank verse', the form preferred by most dramatists in the sixteenth and early seventeenth centuries. It is a very flexible medium, which is capable – like the human speaking voice – of a wide range of tones. Basically, the lines, which are unrhymed, are ten syllables long. The syllables have alternating stresses (one stress followed by one unstressed), just like normal English speech; and they divide into five 'feet'. The technical name for this is 'iambic pentameter'.

Iambic pentameter

> **Solanio**
> Beliéve me, sír, had Í such vénture fórth,
> The bétter párt of my afféctions woúld
> Be wíth my hópes abróad. I shoúld be stíll
> Plúcking the gráss to knów where síts the wínd,
> Píring in máps for pórts, and piérs, and róads;
> And évery óbject thát might máke me feár
> Misfórtune tó my véntures, oút of doúbt
> Would máke me sád.
> **Salarino**
>   My wínd coolíng my bróth
> Would blów me tó an águe whén I thoúght
> What hárm a wínd too gréat might dó at seá.   (1, 1, 15–24)

Here the pentameter accommodates a variety of speech tones – Solanio starts with the simple, conversational expression 'Believe me'; then his speech becomes more dramatic as his imagination takes hold of the subject. Salarino, speaking on the same theme, joins in halfway through a line, as though he were singing the same tune as Solanio.

In this quotation, the lines are fairly regular in length and mostly normal in iambic stress pattern. Solanio's 'every' must be given only two syllables ('ev'ry') as in much modern English speech; and the stresses on 'Plucking' and 'Piring' are not iambic – an irregularity which adds dramatic emphasis.

Sometimes the verse line contains the grammatical unit of meaning – 'Piring in maps for ports, and piers, and roads' – thus allowing for a pause at the end of the line, before a new idea is started; at other times, the sense runs on from one line to the next – 'I should be still / Plucking the grass to know where sits the wind'. This makes for natural fluidity of speech, avoiding monotony but still maintaining the iambic rhythm.

Source, Text, and Date

Popular fiction (see '*The Merchant of Venice*: the Source', p.101) provided the plot outlines, and a rival dramatist's play gave inspiration for the character of Shylock in *The Merchant of Venice*. The play must have been written at some time after June 1596, when an English expedition made a surprise attack on four richly appointed Spanish galleons in Cadiz harbour. In the fighting, these cut adrift and ran aground, and two of them, the *San Matias* and the *San Andrès*, were captured and brought in triumph back to England. It is, almost certainly, this event that Salarino is referring to in Act 1, Scene 1, lines 25–9:

> I should not see the sandy hourglass run
> But I should think of shallows and of flats,
> And see my wealthy Andrew dock'd in sand,
> Vailing her high top lower than her ribs
> To kiss her burial.

The merit of Shakespeare's comedy was already recognized by 1598, when it was praised by Francis Meres in his account of the best contemporary English writing, *Palladis Tamia* (registered for publication September 1598).

The earliest text of the play, published in 1600, was probably based on Shakespeare's own manuscript, and reproduces the author's own detailed (but often imprecise) stage directions. The present edition is based on the text established by M. M. Mahood for the Cambridge Shakespeare in 1987.

the Merchant of Venice

Characters in the Play

The Duke of Venice

The Prince of Morocco
The Prince of Arragon } *suitors to* Portia

Bassanio *an Italian lord, suitor to* Portia

Antonio *a merchant of Venice, friend of* Bassanio

Solanio
Salarino
Gratiano
Lorenzo } *gentlemen of Venice, friends of* Bassanio

Shylock *the rich Jew, a moneylender*

Jessica *his daughter*

Tubal *another Jew, Shylock's friend*

Lancelot Gobbo *servant to* Shylock

Old Gobbo Lancelot's *father*

Portia *a rich Italian lady*

Nerissa *her lady-in-waiting*

Stephano *a messenger*

Leonardo Bassanio's *servant*

Salerio *a messenger from Venice*

Balthazar Portia's *servant*

Jailer

Other serving men, messengers, merchants, officers, court officials, musicians

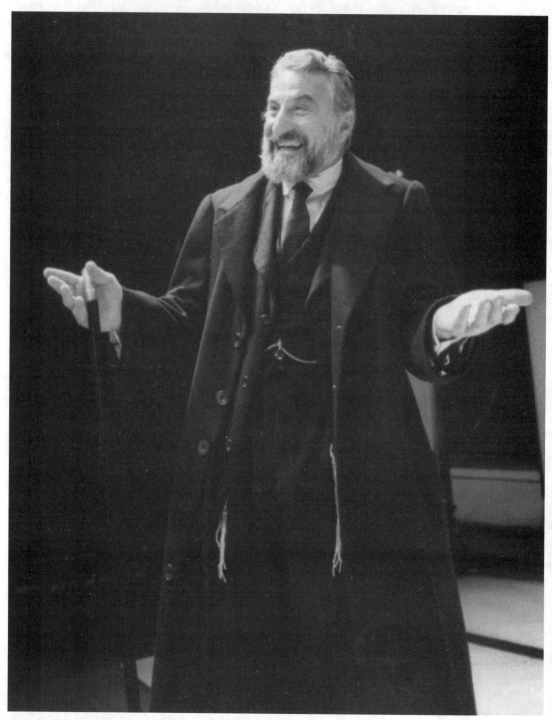

'Rest you fair, good signor! Your worship was the last man in our mouths' (1, 3, 54–5).
Henry Goodman as Shylock, Royal National Theatre, 1999.

ACT 1

Act 1 Scene 1

Antonio is depressed; his friends cannot
cheer him, but he is only too willing to lend
his money to Bassanio.

0s.d. *Salarino*: Some editors print
  'Salerio' here, doubling Antonio's
  business colleague with Portia's
  messenger.
1 *In sooth*: truly.
2 *It*: his sadness.
3 *came by*: got.
5 *am to learn*: do not know.
6 *want-wit*: idiot.
7 *ado*: trouble.
9 *argosies*: merchant ships.
  portly: stately.
10 *signors*: gentleman (the modern
  Italian word is *signori*).
  burghers: citizens.
  flood: sea.
11 *pageants*: decorated carts in carnival
  processions.
12 *overpeer*: look over the heads of.
  petty traffickers: small commercial
  boats.
13 *That . . . reverence*: that bob up and
  down, as if they were showing respect.

15 *had . . . forth*: if I had such business
  abroad.
16 *affections*: concerns.
17 *still*: always.
18 *Plucking . . . wind*: holding up a blade
  of grass to see in which direction the
  wind is blowing.
19 *Piring in*: looking closely at, poring
  over.
  roads: anchorages.
21 *out of doubt*: without doubt.

22 *wind*: breath.
  broth: soup.
23 *ague*: fit of shivering.
25 *sandy hour-glass*: the sands in the
  hour-glass.
26 *shallows*: shallow waters.
  flats: sandbanks.

SCENE 1

Venice: a street. Enter Antonio, Salarino, *and*
Solanio

Antonio
In sooth I know not why I am so sad.
It wearies me, you say it wearies you;
But how I caught it, found it, or came by it,
What stuff 'tis made of, whereof it is born,
5 I am to learn.
And such a want-wit sadness makes of me,
That I have much ado to know myself.
Salarino
Your mind is tossing on the ocean,
There where your argosies with portly sail
10 Like signors and rich burghers on the flood,
Or as it were the pageants of the sea,
Do overpeer the petty traffickers
That curtsy to them, do them reverence,
As they fly by them with their woven wings.
Solanio
15 Believe me, sir, had I such venture forth,
The better part of my affections would
Be with my hopes abroad. I should be still
Plucking the grass to know where sits the wind,
Piring in maps for ports, and piers, and roads;
20 And every object that might make me fear
Misfortune to my ventures, out of doubt
Would make me sad.
Salarino
                            My wind cooling my broth
Would blow me to an ague when I thought
What harm a wind too great might do at sea.
25 I should not see the sandy hourglass run
But I should think of shallows and of flats,

27 *my wealthy Andrew*: my own richly-laden vessel; see 'Source, Date, and Text', p. xxxii.
28 *vailing her high top*: lowering her mast.
   ribs: the wooden sides of the ship.
29 *burial*: burial-ground.
31 *straight*: immediately.
32 *touching but*: only by touching.
   gentle: a) delicate; b) noble.
33–4 *spices . . . silks*: The luxury goods of Venetian trade.
34 *Enrobe*: clothe.
35 *in a word*: briefly.
35–6 *but . . . nothing*: highly valuable just a moment ago, then worth nothing.
36 *thought*: imagination.
38 *such . . . bechanc'd*: such a (disastrous) thing happening.

41 *fortune*: a) wealth; b) luck.

42 *ventures*: business.
   bottom: ship.

44 *fortune*: chance.

46 *Fie, fie*: nonsense; two syllables are missing from this line—perhaps allowing for an embarrassed pause.

And see my wealthy Andrew dock'd in sand,
Vailing her high top lower than her ribs
To kiss her burial. Should I go to church
30 And see the holy edifice of stone
And not bethink me straight of dangerous rocks,
Which touching but my gentle vessel's side
Would scatter all her spices on the stream,
Enrobe the roaring waters with my silks,
35 And (in a word) but even now worth this,
And now worth nothing? Shall I have the thought
To think on this, and shall I lack the thought
That such a thing bechanc'd would make me sad?
But tell not me: I know Antonio
40 Is sad to think upon his merchandise.
   Antonio
Believe me, no. I thank my fortune for it,
My ventures are not in one bottom trusted,
Nor to one place; nor is my whole estate
Upon the fortune of this present year:
45 Therefore my merchandise makes me not sad.
   Solanio
Why then, you are in love.
   Antonio
                              Fie, fie!

50 *Janus*: the two-heading Roman god of doorways and openings, who faced both directions at once.

52 *evermore*: always.
peep . . . eyes: screw up their eyes.
53 *laugh like parrots*: squawk with laughter.
bagpiper: Bagpipes make a melancholy, droning music.

54 *other*: others.
vinegar aspect: sour looks; 'aspect' is stressed on the second syllable.
56 *Nestor*: an old and wise Greek general who fought in the war against Troy.
57 *kinsman*: In Shakespeare's main source, the merchant ('Ansaldo') was the godfather of the younger man ('Giannetto').
61 *prevented*: forestalled, anticipated.
62 *regard*: esteem.
63 *calls on*: needs.
64 *embrace th'occasion*: welcome the opportunity.
66 *laugh*: meet together for fun.
67 *strange*: distant, unfriendly.
68 *We'll . . . yours*: we'll be free when you are.
71 *have in mind*: think about.
72 *I will . . . you*: This half-line could allow Lorenzo some gesture of farewell.

Solanio

Not in love neither? Then let us say you are sad
Because you are not merry; and 'twere as easy
For you to laugh and leap, and say you are merry
50 Because you are not sad. Now by two-headed Janus,
Nature hath fram'd strange fellows in her time:
Some that will evermore peep through their eyes,
And laugh like parrots at a bagpiper;
And other of such vinegar aspect,
55 That they'll not show their teeth in way of smile
Though Nestor swear the jest be laughable.

Enter Bassanio, Lorenzo, *and* Gratiano

Here comes Bassanio, your most noble kinsman,
Gratiano, and Lorenzo. Fare ye well;
We leave you now with better company.

Salarino

60 I would have stay'd till I had made you merry,
If worthier friends had not prevented me.

Antonio

Your worth is very dear in my regard.
I take it your own business calls on you,
And you embrace th'occasion to depart.

Salarino

65 Good morrow, my good lords.

Bassanio

Good signors both, when shall we laugh? Say, when?
You grow exceeding strange; must it be so?

Salarino

We'll make our leisures to attend on yours.

[*Exeunt* Salarino *and* Solanio

Lorenzo

My Lord Bassanio, since you have found Antonio
70 We two will leave you, but at dinner time
I pray you have in mind where we must meet.

Bassanio

I will not fail you.

Gratiano

You look not well, Signor Antonio.

74 *respect upon*: regard for.

75 *They . . . care*: those who worry too much about the world lose the ability to enjoy it.

76 *you . . . chang'd*: you have changed a lot.

77 *hold*: think of.

78 *A stage . . . part*: This Elizabethan commonplace became the motto of Shakespeare's Globe Theatre (*Totus mundus agit histrionem*—all the world plays the actor).

79 *Let . . . Fool*: 'Gratiano' was the name of a comic doctor in the Italian *commedia dell' arte*.

82 *mortifying groans*: Sighing was supposed to shorten life.

84 *his . . . alabaster*: a monumental statue of his grandfather.

85 *Sleep . . . wakes*: be still and silent all day.
jaundice: yellow sickness, thought by the Elizabethans to be of psychological origin.

87 *it is . . . speaks*: I'm saying this because I love you.

88–9 *whose . . . pond*: whose impassive faces are like stagnant ponds filmed over with algae.

90–1 *do . . . opinion*: maintain an obstinate silence in order to get a reputation.

92 *conceit*: thought.

93 *Sir Oracle*: a noble oracle (speaking with divine authority).

94 *ope*: open.
let . . . bark: don't interrupt.

95–7 *know . . . nothing*: know some of these men who are thought to be clever only because they never say anything.

99 *call . . . fools*: 'whosoever shall say to his brother . . . Thou fool, shall be in danger of hell fire' St Matthew, 5:22.

101–2 *fish . . . opinion*: don't use your melancholy to catch yourself an easy and worthless reputation; 'gudgeon' was a particularly gullible fish.

104 *exhortation*: sermon.

108 *moe*: more.

You have too much respect upon the world:
75 They lose it that do buy it with much care.
Believe me, you are marvellously chang'd.

Antonio
I hold the world but as the world, Gratiano:
A stage where every man must play a part,
And mine a sad one.

Gratiano
Let me play the Fool.
80 With mirth and laughter let old wrinkles come,
And let my liver rather heat with wine
Than my heart cool with mortifying groans.
Why should a man whose blood is warm within
Sit like his grandsire cut in alabaster?
85 Sleep when he wakes? And creep into the jaundice
By being peevish? I tell thee what, Antonio—
I love thee, and it is my love that speaks—
There are a sort of men whose visages
Do cream and mantle like a standing pond,
90 And do a wilful stillness entertain,
With purpose to be dress'd in an opinion
Of wisdom, gravity, profound conceit,
As who should say, 'I am Sir Oracle,
And when I ope my lips, let no dog bark!'
95 O my Antonio, I do know of these
That therefore only are reputed wise
For saying nothing; when I am very sure
If they should speak, would almost damn those ears
Which, hearing them, would call their brothers fools.
100 I'll tell thee more of this another time.
But fish not with this melancholy bait
For this fool gudgeon, this opinion.
Come, good Lorenzo. Fare ye well awhile;
I'll end my exhortation after dinner.

Lorenzo
105 Well, we will leave you then till dinner time.
I must be one of these same dumb wise men,
For Gratiano never lets me speak.

Gratiano
Well, keep me company but two years moe,
Thou shalt not know the sound of thine own tongue.

110 *grow . . . gear*: become more talkative for this reason.

112 *a neat's . . . vendible*: an impotent old man and an unmarriageable woman.
neat's tongue: ox-tongue, preserved for eating.
vendible: marketable.
113 *It is . . . now*: peace at last.

115 *reasons*: ideas.

117 *ere*: before.

122–34 *'Tis . . . I owe*: Bassanio is rather inarticulate in his embarrassment.
123 *disabled*: damaged.
124–5 *By . . . continuance*: by flaunting a rather more extravagant lifestyle ('port') than my limited means would allow me to continue.
126 *make . . . abridg'd*: complain about being forced to cut back.
127 *noble rate*: grand style.
care: concern.
128 *come fairly off*: extricate myself honourably.
129 *my time . . . prodigal*: my past, when I was spending rather too lavishly; Bassanio seems to compare himself with the Prodigal Son who spent his inheritance on riotous living (St Luke, chapter 15).
130 *gag'd*: owing.
132 *from . . . warranty*: your love authorizes me.
133 *unburden*: disclose to you.
purposes: plans.
136–7 *if . . . honour*: if your plan looks honourable, as you yourself have always been.
139 *occasions*: needs.
140 *shaft*: arrow.
141 *his fellow . . . flight*: an identical arrow of the same weight ('flight').

Antonio
110 Farewell; I'll grow a talker for this gear.
Gratiano
Thanks, i'faith, for silence is only commendable
In a neat's tongue dried, and a maid not vendible.
[*Exeunt* Gratiano *and* Lorenzo
Antonio
It is that anything now.
Bassanio
Gratiano speaks an infinite deal of nothing, more than
115 any man in all Venice. His reasons are as two grains of
wheat hid in two bushels of chaff: you shall seek all day
ere you find them, and when you have them they are not
worth the search.
Antonio
Well, tell me now what lady is the same
120 To whom you swore a secret pilgrimage
That you today promis'd to tell me of.
Bassanio
'Tis not unknown to you, Antonio,
How much I have disabled mine estate
By something showing a more swelling port
125 Than my faint means would grant continuance.
Nor do I now make moan to be abridg'd
From such a noble rate, but my chief care
Is to come fairly off from the great debts
Wherein my time, something too prodigal,
130 Hath left me gag'd. To you, Antonio,
I owe the most in money and in love,
And from your love I have a warranty
To unburden all my plots and purposes
How to get clear of all the debts I owe.
Antonio
135 I pray you, good Bassanio, let me know it,
And if it stand as you yourself still do
Within the eye of honour, be assur'd
My purse, my person, my extremest means
Lie all unlock'd to your occasions.
Bassanio
140 In my schooldays, when I had lost one shaft,
I shot his fellow of the selfsame flight

142 *advised*: advisèd; careful.

143 *find . . . forth*: to find out where the
other was.
    adventuring: risking.

144 *urge . . . proof*: I'm offering you this
childhood example.

145 *innocence*: ingenuity.

148 *self*: selfsame.

150 *aim*: direction.

150–1 *or . . . Or*: either . . . or.

151 *hazard*: risk, gamble.

152 *rest debtor*: remain in debt.

153 *spend but time*: only waste time.

154 *To . . . circumstance*: in going such a
roundabout way to make use of my
love.

156 *making . . . uttermost*: doubting that I
will give you every assistance.

157 *made waste of*: destroyed.

160 *prest unto*: ready to do.

161 *richly left*: who has inherited a
fortune.

162 *fairer . . . word*: even better than that:
Bassanio sets wealth, beauty, and
virtue in ascending order of
desirability.

163 *Sometimes*: at one time, formerly.

164 *speechless*: unspoken.

165–6 *nothing . . . Portia*: no less worthy
than the historical Portia, daughter of
a distinguished Roman tribune and
the wife of Brutus, who led the
conspiracy against Julius Caesar.

169 *Renowned*: renownèd.
    sunny locks: golden hair.

170 *golden fleece*: In Greek mythology,
Jason led an expedition to Colchis in
search of the golden ram's fleece.

171 *seat*: house.
    strand: shore.

172 *quest*: search.

173–4 *had I . . . them*: if I could become a
rival with these suitors.

175 *presages*: prophesies.
    thrift: profitable success.

176 *questionless*: without doubt.

177 *fortunes*: wealth.

178 *commodity*: merchandise.

The selfsame way, with more advised watch
To find the other forth; and by adventuring both
I oft found both. I urge this childhood proof
145 Because what follows is pure innocence.
I owe you much, and like a wilful youth
That which I owe is lost; but if you please
To shoot another arrow that self way
Which you did shoot the first, I do not doubt,
150 As I will watch the aim, or to find both
Or bring your latter hazard back again
And thankfully rest debtor for the first.
       Antonio
You know me well, and herein spend but time
To wind about my love with circumstance;
155 And out of doubt you do me now more wrong
In making question of my uttermost
Than if you had made waste of all I have.
Then do but say to me what I should do
That in your knowledge may by me be done,
160 And I am prest unto it: therefore speak.
       Bassanio
In Belmont is a lady richly left,
And she is fair, and—fairer than that word—
Of wondrous virtues. Sometimes from her eyes
I did receive fair speechless messages.
165 Her name is Portia, nothing undervalued
To Cato's daughter, Brutus' Portia.
Nor is the wide world ignorant of her worth;
For the four winds blow in from every coast
Renowned suitors, and her sunny locks
170 Hang on her temples like a golden fleece,
Which makes her seat of Belmont Colchos' strand,
And many Jasons come in quest of her.
O my Antonio, had I but the means
To hold a rival place with one of them,
175 I have a mind presages me such thrift
That I should questionless be fortunate.
       Antonio
Thou know'st that all my fortunes are at sea;
Neither have I money nor commodity

179 *a present sum*: some ready money.
180 *Try . . . do*: see what you can borrow
       on my credit in Venice.
181 *rack'd*: stretched.
182 *furnish . . . Belmont*: provide what you
       need to go to Belmont.
183 *presently*: immediately.
184–5 *I . . . sake*: I'm sure you will get it
       either on my credit or for the sake of
       my friendship.

Act 1 Scene 2
Portia is rich, but she has not yet found a
man who can pass her father's test to be
her husband.

  0s.d. *waiting-woman*: lady-in-waiting—a
       companion and confidante.
  1 *troth*: faith.
     aweary: tired; Portia seems to be as
       melancholy as Antonio.
  1–2 *my . . . world*: Portia invokes the
       routine Elizabethan comparison
       between the little human world
       (microcosm) and the physical universe
       (macrocosm).
  4 *in . . . abundance*: as plentiful.
  5 *aught*: anything.
     surfeit: eat excessively.
  6–7 *no mean . . . mean*: no small
       happiness to be set in the middle;
       Nerissa plays on two senses of 'mean'.
  8 *superfluity*: excess.
  9 *competency*: adequacy.
  10 *sentences*: proverbs.
     pronounced: delivered.
  11 *followed*: obeyed.

  12–20 *If . . . cripple*: Portia can provide
       'sentences' of her own.
  13 *had been*: would be.
  14 *divine*: preacher.

  17 *blood*: will, passion; Portia recognizes
       the conflict between head and heart.
  18–20 *such . . . cripple*: crazy young
       love, like a hare, easily eludes the
       snares of well-meaning but unfeeling
       advice.
  20–1 *reasoning . . . husband*: talking like
       this isn't the right way to find myself a
       husband.
  22 *I would*: I like.

To raise a present sum; therefore go forth,
180 Try what my credit can in Venice do,
    That shall be rack'd even to the uttermost
    To furnish thee to Belmont to fair Portia.
    Go presently enquire, and so will I,
    Where money is, and I no question make
185 To have it of my trust or for my sake.   [*Exeunt*

SCENE 2

Belmont: Portia's *house. Enter* Portia *with her
waiting-woman* Nerissa

Portia
By my troth, Nerissa, my little body is aweary of this
great world.
Nerissa
You would be, sweet madam, if your miseries were in
the same abundance as your good fortunes are; and yet
5 for aught I see, they are as sick that surfeit with too
much as they that starve with nothing. It is no mean
happiness, therefore, to be seated in the mean—
superfluity comes sooner by white hairs, but
competency lives longer.
Portia
10 Good sentences, and well pronounced.
Nerissa
They would be better if well followed.
Portia
If to do were as easy as to know what were good to do,
chapels had been churches, and poor men's cottages
princes' palaces. It is a good divine that follows his own
15 instructions; I can easier teach twenty what were good
to be done, than be one of the twenty to follow mine
own teaching. The brain may devise laws for the blood,
but a hot temper leaps o'er a cold decree—such a hare is
madness the youth, to skip o'er the meshes of good
20 counsel the cripple. But this reasoning is not in the
fashion to choose me a husband. O me, the word
'choose'! I may neither choose who I would, nor refuse

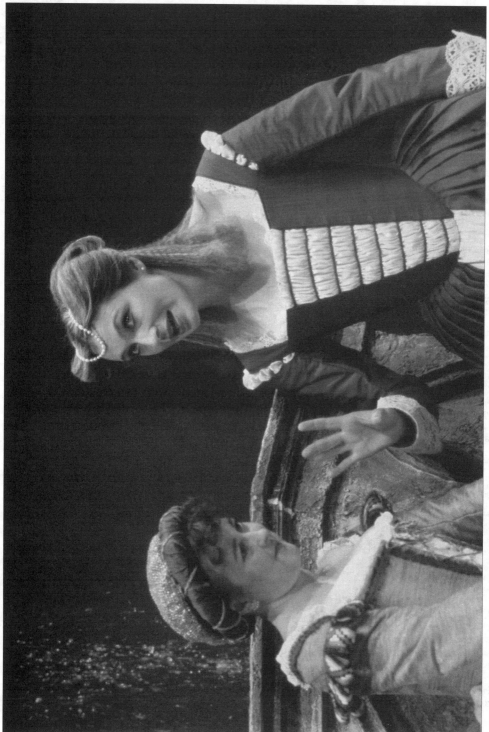

'I may neither choose who I would, nor refuse who I dislike' (*1*, 1, 22–3) Jane Carr as Nerissa and Joanna McCallum as Portia, Chichester Festival Theatre, 1984.

23 *will*: a) wish; b) sexual desire;
c) testament.
curbed: restrained.

26 *ever*: always.

28 *these*: Apparently the caskets are
already on the stage.
29 *his meaning*: the one he intended.
30 *rightly*: a) correctly; b) truly.

34 *over-name*: run through their names.

36 *level*: guess.

37 *Neapolitan*: Portia's suitors are all
national stereotypes.

38 *colt*: uncouth young man.
38–9 *nothing . . . horse*: The southern
Italians were famous for their
horsemanship.
39–40 *appropriation . . . parts*: addition
to his accomplishments.
42 *smith*: blacksmith.

43 *County Palatine*: i.e. a nobleman with
royal privileges, holding jurisdiction
over a province within an empire.
44 *as . . . say*: as if to say.
And: if.
45 *choose*: have it your own way.
46 *prove*: turn out like.
the weeping philosopher: Heraclitus of
Ephesus, who surrendered his throne
and became a melancholy recluse
because he was distressed by human
stupidity.
47 *unmannerly*: impolite, inappropriate.
48 *death's head*: skull.
51 *How . . . by*: what do you think about.

52 *pass for*: be accepted as.

55–6 *he is . . . no man*: he imitates
everybody and is nobody himself.

who I dislike, so is the will of a living daughter curbed
by the will of a dead father. Is it not hard, Nerissa, that I
25 cannot choose one, nor refuse none?

Nerissa
Your father was ever virtuous; and holy men at their
death have good inspirations. Therefore the lottery that
he hath devised in these three chests of gold, silver, and
lead, whereof who chooses his meaning chooses you,
30 will no doubt never be chosen by any rightly but one
who you shall rightly love. But what warmth is there in
your affection towards any of these princely suitors that
are already come?

Portia
I pray thee over-name them, and as thou namest them I
35 will describe them—and according to my description,
level at my affection.

Nerissa
First, there is the Neapolitan prince.

Portia
Ay, that's a colt indeed, for he doth nothing but talk of
his horse; and he makes it a great appropriation to his
40 own good parts that he can shoe him himself. I am
much afeared my lady his mother played false with a
smith.

Nerissa
Then is there the County Palatine.

Portia
He doth nothing but frown, as who should say, 'And you
45 will not have me, choose.' He hears merry tales and
smiles not; I fear he will prove the weeping philosopher
when he grows old, being so full of unmannerly sadness
in his youth. I had rather be married to a death's head
with a bone in his mouth than to either of these. God
50 defend me from these two!

Nerissa
How say you by the French lord, Monsieur Le Bon?

Portia
God made him, and therefore let him pass for a man. In
truth I know it is a sin to be a mocker, but he!—why, he
hath a horse better than the Neapolitan's, a better bad
55 habit of frowning than the Count Palatine: he is every

56 *throstle*: thrush.
56-7 *falls . . . a-capering*: immediately
    begins to dance around.
61 *Falconbridge*: The character of this
    name in Shakespeare's *King John* is a
    model of English conduct.
65 *come . . . court*: bear witness.
66 *have . . . English*: have very little
    knowledge of English.
66-7 *proper man's picture*: the
    appearance of a handsome man.
68 *dumbshow*: mime.
    suited: dressed.

69 *doublet*: sleeveless tunic.
    round hose: padded breeches.
70 *behaviour*: manners.
71 *Scottish*: When James I (James VI of
    Scotland) came to the throne, this was
    discreetly changed to 'other'.
72 *neighbourly charity*: 'Charity worketh
    no ill to his neighbour' (Romans
    13:10).
73 *borrowed . . . of*: received a blow on
    the ear from.
74-6 *the Frenchman . . . another*: the
    Frenchman also promised to repay the
    Englishman for another blow and
    added his signature and seal to the
    (imaginary) bond.
82-3 *fall . . . fell*: befall (= happen) . . .
    befell.
83 *make shift*: contrive.
84 *offer*: attempt.
85 *you . . . perform*: you would be
    refusing to comply with.
88 *Rhenish*: Rhineland; white wine from
    this district was highly esteemed.
    contrary: wrong.

man in no man. If a throstle sing, he falls straight a-capering; he will fence with his own shadow. If I should marry him, I should marry twenty husbands. If he would despise me, I would forgive him; for if he love me to madness, I shall never requite him.

Nerissa

What say you then to Falconbridge, the young baron of England?

Portia

You know I say nothing to him, for he understands not me, nor I him: he hath neither Latin, French, nor Italian, and you will come into the court and swear that I have a poor penny-worth in the English. He is a proper man's picture, but alas who can converse with a dumbshow? How oddly he is suited! I think he bought his doublet in Italy, his round hose in France, his bonnet in Germany, and his behaviour everywhere.

Nerissa

What think you of the Scottish lord his neighbour?

Portia

That he hath a neighbourly charity in him, for he borrowed a box of the ear of the Englishman and swore he would pay him again when he was able. I think the Frenchman became his surety and sealed under for another.

Nerissa

How like you the young German, the Duke of Saxony's nephew!

Portia

Very vilely in the morning when he is sober, and most vilely in the afternoon when he is drunk. When he is best he is a little worse than a man, and when he is worst he is little better than a beast. And the worst fall that ever fell, I hope I shall make shift to go without him.

Nerissa

If he should offer to choose, and choose the right casket, you should refuse to perform your father's will if you should refuse to accept him.

Portia

Therefore, for fear of the worst, I pray thee set a deep glass of Rhenish wine on the contrary casket, for if the

devil be within, and the temptation without, I know he
90 will choose it. I will do anything, Nerissa, ere I will be
married to a sponge.

Nerissa

You need not fear, lady, the having any of these lords.
They have acquainted me with their determinations,
which is indeed to return to their home, and to trouble
95 you with no more suit unless you may be won by some
other sort than your father's imposition, depending on
the caskets.

Portia

If I live to be as old as Sibylla, I will die as chaste as
Diana unless I be obtained by the manner of my father's
100 will. I am glad this parcel of wooers are so reasonable,
for there is not one among them but I dote on his very
absence; and I pray God grant them a fair departure.

Nerissa

Do you not remember, lady, in your father's time, a
Venetian, a scholar and a soldier, that came hither in
105 company of the Marquis of Montferrat?

Portia

Yes, yes, it was Bassanio!—as I think so was he called.

Nerissa

True, madam; he of all the men that ever my foolish eyes
looked upon was the best deserving a fair lady.

Portia

I remember him well, and I remember him worthy of
110 thy praise.

Enter a Servingman

How now, what news?

Servingman

The four strangers seek for you, madam, to take their
leave; and there is a forerunner come from a fifth, the
Prince of Morocco, who brings word the prince his
115 master will be here tonight.

Portia

If I could bid the fifth welcome with so good heart as I
can bid the other four farewell, I should be glad of his
approach. If he have the condition of a saint, and the

---

**Side notes (left column):**

92 *the having*: having to accept.
93 *determinations*: decisions.

96 *sort*: means, way.

98 *Sibylla*: In classical mythology the sibyl (= prophetess) of Cumae was granted as many years of life as she could hold grains of sand in her hand.
99 *Diana*: the classical goddess of chastity.
100 *parcel*: bunch.

104 *a scholar . . . soldier*: This was the Renaissance idea of a perfect man.
105 *Marquis of Montferrat*: The contemporary holder of this title was the Duke of Mantua, who had fought against the Turks in 1595.
106 *as I think*: Portia attempts to conceal her interest.

112 *four*: Shakespeare probably forgot that there were *six* suitors.
113 *forerunner*: herald.

118 *condition*: character, disposition.

119 *complexion*: appearance.
119–20 *I had . . . wive me*: would rather have him for a priest than a husband.
119 *shrive*: give absolution (after confession).

Shylock will lend the money—but he demands an unusual bond.

1 *ducats*: Venetian gold coins.

5 *bound*: as security.

6 *stead*: supply.
pleasure: oblige.

11 *good*: financially secure; but Bassanio takes the word to mean 'honourable'.

14 *sufficient*: adequate security.

15 *in supposition*: to be assumed.
argosy: merchant ship.

17 *the Rialto*: the Venetian Stock Exchange.

19 *squandered*: scattered lavishly.

complexion of a devil, I had rather he should shrive me
120 than wive me.
Come, Nerissa; sirrah, go before:
Whiles we shut the gate upon one wooer, another
        knocks at the door.   [*Exeunt*

Scene 3

Venice: a public place. Enter Bassanio *with* Shylock
the Jew

Shylock
Three thousand ducats, well.
Bassanio
Ay, sir, for three months.
Shylock
For three months, well.
Bassanio
For the which, as I told you, Antonio shall be bound.
Shylock
5 Antonio shall become bound, well.
Bassanio
May you stead me? Will you pleasure me? Shall I know
your answer?
Shylock
Three thousand ducats for three months, and Antonio
bound.
Bassanio
10 Your answer to that?
Shylock
Antonio is a good man—
Bassanio
Have you heard any imputation to the contrary?
Shylock
Ho no, no, no, no: my meaning in saying he is a good
man is to have you understand me that he is sufficient.
15 Yet his means are in supposition: he hath an argosy
bound to Tripolis, another to the Indies; I understand
moreover upon the Rialto he hath a third at Mexico, a
fourth for England, and other ventures he hath
squandered abroad. But ships are but boards, sailors but

20 men; there be land rats, and water rats, water thieves
and land thieves—I mean pirates—and then there is
the peril of waters, winds, and rocks. The man is
notwithstanding sufficient. Three thousand ducats: I
think I may take his bond.

Bassanio

25 Be assured you may.

Shylock

I will be assured I may; and that I may be assured, I will
bethink me—may I speak with Antonio?

Bassanio

If it please you to dine with us—

Shylock

Yes, to smell pork, to eat of the habitation which your
30 prophet the Nazarite conjured the devil into. I will buy
with you, sell with you, talk with you, walk with you,
and so following; but I will not eat with you, drink with
you, nor pray with you. What news on the Rialto? Who
is he comes here?

Enter Antonio

Bassanio

35 This is Signor Antonio.

Shylock

[*Aside*] How like a fawning publican he looks!
I hate him for he is a Christian;
But more, for that in low simplicity
He lends out money gratis, and brings down
40 The rate of usance here with us in Venice.
If I can catch him once upon the hip,
I will feed fat the ancient grudge I bear him.
He hates our sacred nation, and he rails
Even there where merchants most do congregate
45 On me, my bargains, and my well-won thrift
Which he calls interest. Curs'd be my tribe
If I forgive him!

Bassanio   Shylock, do you hear?

Shylock

I am debating of my present store,

---

21 *pirates*: These were terrorists to shipping in the Adriatic.

25, 26 *assured*: a) reassured; b) financially secure.

27 *bethink me*: give the matter some consideration.

29 *pork*: A meat forbidden to the Jews.
29–30 *the habitation . . . into*: Jesus of Nazareth ('the Nazarite') ordered the devils possessing the mind of a madman to enter into a herd of pigs (St Mark 5:1–13).
32 *and so following*: etcetera.

36 *fawning publican*: servile tax-collector.
37 *for*: because.
38 *low simplicity*: humble foolishness.
39 *gratis*: interest-free.
40 *usance*: usury, money-lending.
41 *upon the hip*: at a disadvantage.

43 *rails*: speaks abuse.

45 *bargains*: business deals.
   thrift: success.
46 *interest*: profit.

48 *debating of*: reckoning up.
   present store: ready money.

49 *near*: close.
50 *gross*: whole sum.

53 *furnish*: supply.
   soft: wait a minute.
55 *in our mouths*: that we were talking about.
56 *albeit*: although.
57 *excess*: interest, anything above the sum lent.
58 *ripe*: pressing, urgent.
59 *possess'd*: informed.
60 *would*: want.

65 *Upon advantage*: with interest.
   I . . . use it: I never do so.

66–83 *When Jacob . . . Jacob's*: Shylock conflates two stories: Genesis 27 tells how Jacob, with the help of 'his wise mother', tricked his brother out of his birthright; and Genesis 30 describes the deception of Laban as Shylock recounts it here.
66 *graz'd*: shepherded.
67 *our holy Abram*: The patriarch Abraham was the founder of the Jewish race.
68 *wrought*: devised.
73 *compromis'd*: agreed.
74 *eanlings*: new-born lambs.
   streak'd and pied: with fleeces of two colours.
75 *fall as Jacob's hire*: be counted as Jacob's wages.
   rank: on heat, ready for mating.
76 *turned*: turnèd.
77 *work of generation*: mating.

And by the near guess of my memory
50 I cannot instantly raise up the gross
Of full three thousand ducats. What of that?
Tubal, a wealthy Hebrew of my tribe,
Will furnish me. But soft, how many months
Do you desire? [*To* Antonio] Rest you fair, good signor!
55 Your worship was the last man in our mouths.
  Antonio
Shylock, albeit I neither lend nor borrow
By taking nor by giving of excess,
Yet to supply the ripe wants of my friend
I'll break a custom. [*To* Bassanio] Is he yet possess'd
60 How much ye would?
  Shylock
                    Ay, ay, three thousand ducats.
  Antonio
And for three months.
  Shylock
I had forgot, three months; [*To* Bassanio] you told me so.
Well then, your bond; and let me see—but hear you,
Methoughts you said you neither lend nor borrow
65 Upon advantage.
  Antonio
                  I do never use it.
  Shylock
When Jacob graz'd his uncle Laban's sheep—
This Jacob from our holy Abram was
(As his wise mother wrought in his behalf)
The third possessor; ay, he was the third—
  Antonio
70 And what of him, did he take interest?
  Shylock
No, not take interest, not as you would say
Directly interest. Mark what Jacob did:
When Laban and himself were compromis'd
That all the eanlings which were streak'd and pied
75 Should fall as Jacob's hire, the ewes being rank
In end of autumn turned to the rams,
And when the work of generation was
Between these woolly breeders in the act,

79 *pill'd . . . wands*: went and stripped
   the bark of some twigs; 'me' is used
   purely for emphasis.
80 *deed of kind*: act of breeding.
81 *fulsome*: passionate.
82 *eaning*: lambing.
83 *Fall*: gave birth to.
85 *thrift*: profit.
86 *venture*: speculation; Antonio
   approves Jacob's calculated
   enterprise.
   serv'd for: worked for; usury was
   condemned partly because no work
   was involved.
88 *sway'd*: governed.
   fashion'd: shaped.
89 *Was . . . good*: did you bring up this
   story as a justification of usury.
93 *cite*: quote.
100 *beholding*: indebted.

101 *oft*: often.
102 *rated*: scolded.
103 *usances*: financial deals.
104 *Still*: always.
105 *suff'rance*: long-suffering,
    forebearance.
    badge: a) characteristic;
    b) distinguishing mark: Venetian Jews
    at this time were compelled to wear a
    yellow O.
106 *misbeliever*: heretic, unbeliever.
    dog: The Jews believed that dogs were
    unclean.
107 *gaberdine*: long loose coat, worn
    traditionally by Jews.
110 *Go to, then*: and now what are you
    doing (an expression of exasperation).
111 *monies*: The plural form may be
    Shakespeare's attempt to indicate
    some Jewish speech habit.
112 *void your rheum*: spit.

The skilful shepherd pill'd me certain wands
80 And in the doing of the deed of kind
He stuck them up before the fulsome ewes,
Who then conceiving, did in eaning time
Fall parti-coloured lambs, and those were Jacob's.
This was a way to thrive, and he was blest;
85 And thrift is blessing if men steal it not.
   Antonio
This was a venture, sir, that Jacob serv'd for,
A thing not in his power to bring to pass,
But sway'd and fashion'd by the hand of heaven.
Was this inserted to make interest good?
90 Or is your gold and silver ewes and rams?
   Shylock
I cannot tell, I make it breed as fast.
But note me, signor—
   Antonio
                    Mark you this, Bassanio,
The devil can cite Scripture for his purpose.
An evil soul producing holy witness
95 Is like a villain with a smiling cheek,
A goodly apple rotten at the heart.
O what a goodly outside falsehood hath!
   Shylock
Three thousand ducats, 'tis a good round sum.
Three months from twelve, then let me see, the rate—
   Antonio
100 Well, Shylock, shall we be beholding to you?
   Shylock
Signor Antonio, many a time and oft
In the Rialto you have rated me
About my monies and my usances.
Still have I borne it with a patient shrug
105 For suff'rance is the badge of all our tribe.
You call me misbeliever, cut-throat dog,
And spit upon my Jewish gaberdine,
And all for use of that which is mine own.
Well then, it now appears you need my help.
110 Go to, then, you come to me, and you say,
'Shylock, we would have monies'—you say so,
You that did void your rheum upon my beard,

113 *foot*: kick.
114 *suit*: request.

118 *key*: tone.
119 *With bated breath*: anxiously.
120 *Say this*: The pause in the line,
allowing time for a gesture of mock-
humility, throws emphasis on
Shylock's conclusion.

125 *as like*: just as likely.

129 *A breed . . . friend*: an increase in the
sum of sterile money from a friend.

131 *break*: go bankrupt.

136 *doit*: a Dutch coin of little value.
137 *usance*: interest.
138 *kind*: kindness; Bassanio takes the
word in its normal sense—but Shylock
will pun on the meaning 'natural
inclination'.

140 *notary*: solicitor.
   seal me: sign for me.
141 *single*: simple.
   in a merry sport: as a joke.

144 *the condition*: the terms of the bond.
145 *nominated for*: named as.
   equal: exact.

And foot me as you spurn a stranger cur
Over your threshold: monies is your suit.
115 What should I say to you? Should I not say
'Hath a dog money? Is it possible
A cur can lend three thousand ducats?' Or
Shall I bend low, and in a bondman's key,
With bated breath and whisp'ring humbleness,
120 Say this:
'Fair sir, you spat on me on Wednesday last,
You spurn'd me such a day, another time
You call'd me dog: and for these courtesies
I'll lend you thus much monies.'
        Antonio
125 I am as like to call thee so again,
To spit on thee again, to spurn thee too.
If thou wilt lend this money, lend it not
As to thy friends, for when did friendship take
A breed for barren metal of his friend?
130 But lend it rather to thine enemy,
Who if he break, thou mayst with better face
Exact the penalty.
        Shylock
Why look you how you storm!
I would be friends with you, and have your love,
135 Forget the shames that you have stain'd me with,
Supply your present wants, and take no doit
Of usance for my monies, and you'll not hear me.
This is kind I offer.
        Bassanio
                This were kindness.
        Shylock
This kindness will I show.
140 Go with me to a notary, seal me there
Your single bond, and, in a merry sport,
If you repay me not on such a day,
In such a place, such sum or sums as are
Express'd in the condition, let the forfeit
145 Be nominated for an equal pound
Of your fair flesh, to be cut off and taken
In what part of your body pleaseth me.

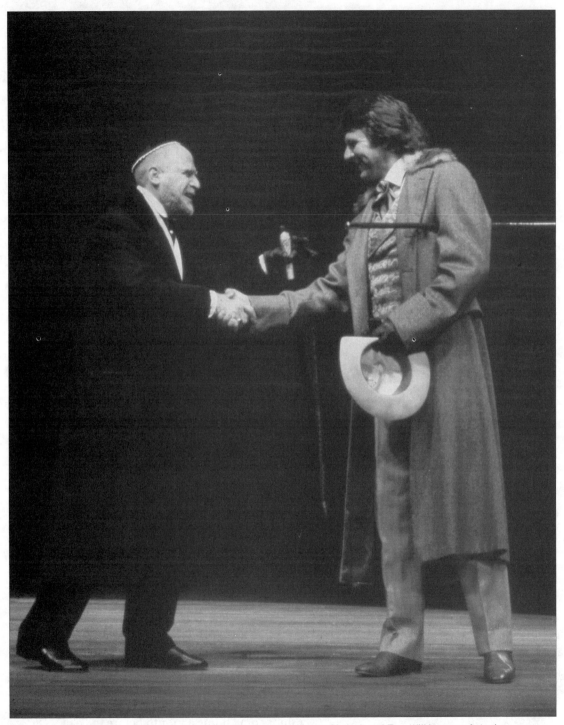

'Yes, Shylock, I will seal unto this bond.' (*1*, 3, 167). David Suchet as Shylock and Tom Wilkinson as Antonio, Royal Shakespeare Company, 1981.

Antonio
Content, in faith! I'll seal to such a bond,
And say there is much kindness in the Jew.
Bassanio
150 You shall not seal to such a bond for me;
I'll rather dwell in my necessity.
Antonio
Why, fear not, man, I will not forfeit it.
Within these two months, that's a month before
This bond expires, I do expect return
155 Of thrice three times the value of this bond.
Shylock
O father Abram, what these Christians are,
Whose own hard dealings teaches them suspect
The thoughts of others! Pray you tell me this:
If he should break his day what should I gain
160 By the exaction of the forfeiture?
A pound of man's flesh, taken from a man,
Is not so estimable, profitable neither,
As flesh of muttons, beefs, or goats. I say
To buy his favour, I extend this friendship.
165 If he will take it, so; if not, adieu,
And for my love, I pray you wrong me not.
Antonio
Yes, Shylock, I will seal unto this bond.
Shylock
Then meet me forthwith at the notary's.
Give him direction for this merry bond,
170 And I will go and purse the ducats straight,
See to my house left in the fearful guard
Of an unthrifty knave, and presently
I'll be with you.   [*Exit*
Antonio
                    Hie thee, gentle Jew.
The Hebrew will turn Christian, he grows kind.
Bassanio
175 I like not fair terms and a villain's mind.
Antonio
Come on, in this there can be no dismay,
My ships come home a month before the day.
                                                    [*Exeunt*

151 *dwell . . . necessity*: remain in need; Bassanio emphasizes his meaning with his rhyme.

157 *hard*: tough.
suspect: to be suspicious.

159 *break his day*: fail to pay on the agreed date.

163 *muttons, beefs*: sheep, oxen; Shylock's usage seems to emphasize his status as an 'outsider'.

170 *purse . . . straight*: get the money ready immediately.
171 *fearful*: untrustworthy.
172 *unthrifty*: careless.
knave: lad, servant.

173 *gentle*: Antonio makes a pun with 'Gentile' (= a non-Jewish person).

ACT 2

Os.d. *flourish*: fanfare.
Os.d. *a tawny Moor . . . accordingly*: The
　details and the vagueness about
　numbers, are typical of an author's
　own manuscript.
　accordingly: in the same way.
1–3 *Mislike . . . bred*: 'Marvel not at me
　that I am so black, for why? the sun
　hath shined upon me' (Song of
　Solomon).
1 *Mislike*: dislike.
2 *shadow'd*: darkened.
　livery: uniform.
3 *near bred*: closely related.
4 *fairest*: most light-skinned.
5 *Phoebus*: the god of the sun.
6 *make incision*: cut ourselves.
7 *reddest*: Red blood showed courage.
8 *aspect*: aspèct.
9 *fear'd*: terrified.
10 *best-regarded*: most admired.
　clime: part of the world.
12 *steal your thoughts*: win your
　affections.

13 *In . . . choice*: when it comes to
　choosing.
　led: influenced.
14 *nice*: fastidious, over-particular.
16 *Bars*: forbids.

17 *scanted*: restricted.

18 *hedg'd*: confined.
18–19 *to yield . . . wife*: marry that man.

20 *renowned*: renownèd.
　then . . . fair: would then have stood
　as good a chance; Portia plays on
　'fair' = light-skinned.
21 *any comer*: any other suitor.

24 *scimitar*: short curved sword.

SCENE 1

Belmont: Portia*'s house. A flourish of cornets. Enter
the* Prince of Morocco, *a tawny Moor all in white,
and three or four followers accordingly; with* Portia,
Nerissa, *and their train*

Morocco
Mislike me not for my complexion,
The shadow'd livery of the burnish'd sun,
To whom I am a neighbour and near bred.
Bring me the fairest creature northward born,
5　Where Phoebus' fire scarce thaws the icicles,
And let us make incision for your love
To prove whose blood is reddest, his or mine.
I tell thee, lady, this aspect of mine
Hath fear'd the valiant; by my love I swear
10　The best-regarded virgins of our clime
Have lov'd it too. I would not change this hue,
Except to steal your thoughts, my gentle queen.
　Portia
In terms of choice I am not solely led
By nice direction of a maiden's eyes.
15　Besides, the lottery of my destiny
Bars me the right of voluntary choosing.
But if my father had not scanted me,
And hedg'd me by his wit to yield myself
His wife who wins me by that means I told you,
20　Yourself, renowned prince, then stood as fair
As any comer I have looked on yet
For my affection.
　Morocco
　　　　　　　Even for that I thank you.
Therefore I pray you lead me to the caskets
To try my fortune. By this scimitar,

25–6 *slew . . . Solyman*: The Moroccans owed allegiance to the Turks who, under Solyman the Magnificent, fought against the Persians in the mid-sixteenth century—but no Shah ('Sophy') was killed in the fighting.
26 *fields*: battlefields, battles.
   of: over.
27 *o'er-stare*: outface, defy.
30 *a roars*: he roars.
32 *Hercules and Lichas*: In classical mythology, the superman (grandson of Alceus) and his servant.
   play at dice: toss dice, gamble.
35 *So . . . rage*: just as Hercules was destroyed by his own frenzy.

25 That slew the Sophy and a Persian prince
   That won three fields of Sultan Solyman,
   I would o'er-stare the sternest eyes that look,
   Outbrave the heart most daring on the earth,
   Pluck the young sucking cubs from the she-bear,
30 Yea, mock the lion when a roars for prey,
   To win thee, lady. But alas the while,
   If Hercules and Lichas play at dice
   Which is the better man, the greater throw
   May turn by fortune from the weaker hand.
35 So is Alcides beaten by his rage,
   And so may I, blind Fortune leading me,
   Miss that which one unworthier may attain,
   And die with grieving.

   Portia
                          You must take your chance,
   And either not attempt to choose at all

42 *In way of*: on the subject of.
   be advis'd: consider, be careful.

40 Or swear before you choose, if you choose wrong,
   Never to speak to lady afterward
   In way of marriage: therefore be advis'd.

43 *Nor will not*: I certainly won't.
   chance: fate, trial.

   Morocco
   Nor will not. Come, bring me unto my chance.

   Portia
   First forward to the temple; after dinner

44 *forward . . . temple*: Oaths of such magnitude were customarily taken at an altar.

45 Your hazard shall be made.

   Morocco
                          Good fortune then,
   To make me blest—or cursed'st among men!

46 *cursed*: cursèd.
46s.d. *Cornets*: Another fanfare to mark the Prince's departure.

   Cornets.   [*Exeunt*

Act 2 Scene 2
Lancelot Gobbo teases his blind father, who asks Bassanio to give employment to his son. Bassanio is preparing for Belmont, and Gratiano wants to accompany him.

0s.d. *Scene 2*: The action of Scenes 2–6 can be made continuous, provided that the three stage entrances are clearly identified—the door of Shylock's house, the direction of Gratiano's lodging, and the opening (perhaps the central, curtained space) for Bassanio's house.

0s.d. *the Clown*: An indication that the part was played by the company's professional comedian (Will Kemp).

1 *serve me*: a) assist me; b) obey me.

2 *The fiend*: the devil; Lancelot imagines himself as the central character of a Morality Play.

8 *scorn*: despise—with a play on the sense 'kick aside'.

9 *courageous*: encouraging.
   pack: be gone.
   Fia: on your way (Italian).

12 *hanging . . . heart*: clinging to my heart.

14 *honest woman*: virtuous woman.

15–16 *my father . . . taste*: Lancelot hints at his father's sexual activities.

17 *budge*: move, leave.

21 *God . . . mark*: if I may say so; Lancelot apologizes for his language.

23 *saving your reverence*: if you'll excuse me.

24 *incarnation*: incarnate; mistaken words ('malapropisms') are Will Kemp's speciality.

25 *in my conscience*: to speak truly.

26 *hard*: strict.
   offer: presume.

Scene 2

Venice: the street outside Shylock's house. Enter
Lancelot Gobbo, *the Clown, alone*

Lancelot

Certainly, my conscience will serve me to run from this Jew my master. The fiend is at mine elbow and tempts me, saying to me 'Gobbo, Lancelot Gobbo, good Lancelot', or 'Good Gobbo', or 'Good Lancelot Gobbo,
5 use your legs, take the start, run away.' My conscience says 'No: take heed, honest Lancelot, take heed, honest Gobbo'—or (as aforesaid)—'honest Lancelot Gobbo; do not run, scorn running with thy heels.' Well, the most courageous fiend bids me pack. 'Fia!' says the fiend,
10 'Away!' says the fiend. ''For the heavens, rouse up a brave mind', says the fiend, 'and run.' Well, my conscience, hanging about the neck of my heart, says very wisely to me, 'My honest friend Lancelot, being an honest man's son, or rather an honest woman's son' (for
15 indeed my father did something smack, something grow to; he had a kind of taste): well, my conscience says 'Lancelot, budge not!' 'Budge!' says the fiend. 'Budge not!' says my conscience. 'Conscience', say I, 'you counsel well.' 'Fiend', say I, 'you counsel well'. To be
20 ruled by my conscience, I should stay with the Jew my master who—God bless the mark!—is a kind of devil; and to run away from the Jew, I should be ruled by the fiend who—saving your reverence—is the devil himself. Certainly the Jew is the very devil incarnation,
25 and, in my conscience, my conscience is but a kind of hard conscience to offer to counsel me to stay with the Jew. The fiend gives the more friendly counsel: I will run, fiend, my heels are at your commandment, I will run.

Enter Old Gobbo *with a basket*

Gobbo

30 Master young-man, you, I pray you, which is the way to Master Jew's?

'Master young-gentleman, I pray you, which is the way to Master Jew's?' (*2*, 2, 35–6). Rob Edwards as Lancelot Gobbo and Jimmy Gardner as Old Gobbo, Royal Shakespeare Company, 1981.

32 *true-begotten father*: Another
deliberate confusion.
33 *sand-blind*: half-blind.
high . . . blind: almost stone
(= completely) blind.
34 *try confusions*: test him out, give him
some riddles.

37–40 *Turn . . . house*: This is an old
joke, made more effective if Lancelot
turns his father about until he faces
Shylock's door.
38 *Marry*: by the Virgin Mary (a mild
oath).
41 *Be . . . sonties*: by God's saints; Old
Gobbo speaks a rural dialect.
hit: find.
42 *one*: a certain.
dwells with him: is a member of his
household.
42–3 *dwell with him*: lives with him.
45 *raise the waters*: bring tears to his
eyes.

49 *well to live*: well-to-do, prosperous;
another malapropism.

50 *a*: he.

52 *Your . . . Lancelot*: just call him plain
Lancelot.

55 *an't*: if it.

56 *ergo*: therefore; Lancelot wants to
confuse his father with the Latin word.
57 *father*: A courteous way of addressing
an old man—making for more comedy
here.
58 *sisters three*: The Fates—three sister-
goddesses of classical mythology who
controlled human destiny.

Lancelot

[*Aside*] O heavens! This is my true-begotten father who
being more than sand-blind, high gravel-blind, knows
me not. I will try confusions with him.

Gobbo

35 Master young-gentleman, I pray you, which is the way
to Master Jew's?

Lancelot

Turn upon your right hand at the next turning, but at
the next turning of all on your left. Marry, at the very
next turning turn of no hand but turn down indirectly
40 to the Jew's house.

Gobbo

Be God's sonties, 'twill be a hard way to hit! Can you tell
me whether one Lancelot that dwells with him, dwell
with him or no?

Lancelot

Talk you of young Master Lancelot? [*Aside*] Mark me
45 now, now will I raise the waters. Talk you of young
Master Lancelot?

Gobbo

No 'master', sir, but a poor man's son. His father, though
I say't, is an honest, exceeding poor man and, God be
thanked, well to live.

Lancelot

50 Well, let his father be what a will, we talk of young
Master Lancelot.

Gobbo

Your worship's friend and Lancelot, sir.

Lancelot

But I pray you, *ergo* old man, *ergo* I beseech you, talk
you of young Master Lancelot?

Gobbo

55 Of Lancelot, an't please your mastership.

Lancelot

Ergo Master Lancelot. Talk not of Master Lancelot,
father, for the young gentleman, according to fates and
destinies, and such odd sayings, the sisters three, and
such branches of learning, is indeed deceased, or as you
60 would say in plain terms, gone to heaven.

63 *hovel-post*: main timber support of
   poor dwelling.

71–2 *a wise . . . child*: Lancelot inverts
   the proverb 'It is a wise child that
   knows his own father'.

88 *thou*: Old Gobbo shifts from the
   respectful form 'you' to the familiar
   form of address.
86–7 *Lord . . . be*: the Lord be praised.
87 *what . . . got*: Old Gobbo (unaware
   that his son is kneeling) has grasped
   the hair of Lancelot's head.
89 *fill-horse*: carthorse ('fills' = the shafts
   of a cart).

Gobbo

Marry, God forbid! The boy was the very staff of my age, my very prop.

Lancelot

Do I look like a cudgel or a hovel-post, a staff or a prop? Do you know me, father?

Gobbo

65 Alack the day, I know you not, young gentleman, but I pray you tell me, is my boy—God rest his soul!—alive or dead?

Lancelot

Do you not know me, father?

Gobbo

Alack, sir, I am sand-blind, I know you not.

Lancelot

70 Nay indeed, if you had your eyes you might fail of the knowing me: it is a wise father that knows his own child. Well, old man, I will tell you news of your son. [*Kneels*] Give me your blessing; truth will come to light, murder cannot be hid long, a man's son may, but in the 75 end truth will out.

Gobbo

Pray you, sir, stand up; I am sure you are not Lancelot my boy.

Lancelot

Pray you, let's have no more fooling about it, but give me your blessing; I am Lancelot your boy that was, your 80 son that is, your child that shall be.

Gobbo

I cannot think you are my son.

Lancelot

I know not what I shall think of that; but I am Lancelot the Jew's man, and I am sure Margery your wife is my mother.

Gobbo

85 Her name is Margery indeed. I'll be sworn if thou be Lancelot thou art mine own flesh and blood. Lord worshipped might he be, what a beard hast thou got! Thou has got more hair on thy chin than Dobbin my fill-horse has on his tail.

90 *backward*: i.e. shorter.

91 *of*: on.

94 *agree*: suit each other.
'gree: agree.

96 *for . . . part*: so far as I am concerned.
96–7 *set . . . rest*: made up my mind;
'rest' = final gambling stake.
98 *ground*: distance.
very: real (an intensifier).
99 *halter*: rope (to hang himself).
100 *tell . . . ribs*: count all my ribs with
your fingers; traditionally, Lancelot
puts his father's hand on his own
fingers, spread out to represent his
ribs.
101 *give . . . present*: give your present on
my behalf.
102 *rare new liveries*: splendid fashionable
uniforms.
104–5 *a Jew*: i.e. 'someone I could not
possibly be' (compare the modern 'I'm
a Dutchman').

106 *hasted*: speeded up.

108 *put . . . making*: get the uniforms
made.
109 *anon*: at once.

110 *To him*: speak to him.

112 *Gramercy*: may God reward you
(derived from Old French *grant merci*).

Lancelot

90 It should seem then that Dobbin's tail grows backward.
I am sure he had more hair of his tail than I have of my
face when I last saw him.

Gobbo

Lord, how art thou changed! How dost thou and thy
master agree? I have brought him a present. How 'gree

95 you now?

Lancelot

Well, well; but for mine own part, as I have set up my
rest to run away, so I will not rest till I have run some
ground. My master's a very Jew. Give him a present?
Give him a halter! I am famished in his service; you may

100 tell every finger I have with my ribs. Father, I am glad
you are come; give me your present to one Master
Bassanio, who indeed gives rare new liveries: if I serve
not him, I will run as far as God has any ground. O rare
fortune, here comes the man! To him, father, for I am a

105 Jew if I serve the Jew any longer.

Enter Bassanio *with* Leonardo *and a follower or two*

Bassanio

You may do so, but let it be so hasted that supper be
ready at the farthest by five of the clock. See these letters
delivered, put the liveries to making, and desire
Gratiano to come anon to my lodging.

[Exit one of his men

Lancelot

110 To him, father.

Gobbo

God bless your worship!

Bassanio

Gramercy; wouldst thou aught with me?

Gobbo

Here's my son, sir, a poor boy—

Lancelot

Not a poor boy, sir, but the rich Jew's man that would,

115 sir, as my father shall specify—

116 *infection*: Gobbo's mistake for 'affection' (= desire).

118 *the short and long*: all that needs to be said; Lancelot inverts the usual phrase.

120 *saving . . . reverence*: if you'll allow me to say this.
121 *cater-cousins*: close friends who eat together.

124 *frutify*: Lancelot combines 'notify' and 'fructify' (= bear fruit)—which Old Gobbo takes as the cue for his gift.
125 *dish of doves*: doves prepared for eating.

127 *impertinent*: Lancelot means 'pertinent' (= relevant).
132 *defect*: i.e. 'effect' (= purpose).
133 *thou . . . suit*: your request is granted.
135 *preferr'd*: recommended.
preferment: promotion.
138 *old proverb*: 'The grace of God is gear enough (for salvation)'.
parted: divided.
142–3 *enquire . . . out*: make your way to my house.

144 *more guarded*: with more (gold) braid; the extra trimmings might suggest that Lancelot is to act as a jester.

Gobbo
He hath a great infection, sir, as one would say, to serve—
Lancelot
Indeed, the short and the long is, I serve the Jew, and have a desire, as my father shall specify—
Gobbo
120 His master and he, saving your worship's reverence, are scarce cater-cousins—
Lancelot
To be brief, the very truth is that the Jew having done me wrong doth cause me—as my father being I hope an old man shall frutify unto you—
Gobbo
125 I have here a dish of doves that I would bestow upon your worship, and my suit is—
Lancelot
In very brief, the suit is impertinent to myself, as your worship shall know by this honest old man, and though I say it, though old man, yet poor man, my father—
Bassanio
130 One speak for both. What would you?
Lancelot
Serve you, sir.
Gobbo
That is the very defect of the matter, sir.
Bassanio
I know thee well, thou hast obtain'd thy suit.
Shylock thy master spoke with me this day,
135 And hath preferr'd thee, if it be preferment
To leave a rich Jew's service to become
The follower of so poor a gentleman.
Lancelot
The old proverb is very well parted between my master Shylock and you, sir: you have the grace of God, sir, and
140 he hath enough.
Bassanio
Thou speak'st it well; go, father, with thy son;
Take leave of thy old master, and enquire
My lodging out. [*To a follower*] Give him a livery
More guarded than his fellows'; see it done.

Lancelot

145 Father, in. I cannot get a service, no, I have ne'er a
tongue in my head! [*Looks at palm of his hand*] Well, if
any man in Italy have a fairer table which doth offer to
swear upon a book!—I shall have good fortune. Go to,
here's a simple line of life, here's a small trifle of wives:
150 alas, fifteen wives is nothing, eleven widows and nine
maids is a simple coming-in for one man. And then to
'scape drowning thrice, and to be in peril of my life with
the edge of a featherbed: here are simple 'scapes. Well, if
Fortune be a woman, she's a good wench for this gear.
155 Father, come, I'll take my leave of the Jew in the
twinkling.   [*Exeunt* Lancelot *and* Gobbo

Bassanio

I pray thee, good Leonardo, think on this.
These things being bought and orderly bestow'd,
Return in haste, for I do feast tonight
160 My best esteem'd acquaintance. Hie thee, go.

Leonardo

My best endeavours shall be done herein.

Enter Gratiano

Gratiano

Where's your master?

Leonardo

                              Yonder, sir, he walks.   [*Exit*

Gratiano

Signor Bassanio!

Bassanio

Gratiano?

Gratiano

165 I have a suit to you.

Bassanio

                              You have obtain'd it.

Gratiano

You must not deny me, I must go with you to Belmont.

Bassanio

Why then, you must. But hear thee, Gratiano:
Thou art too wild, too rude, and bold of voice—
Parts that become thee happily enough,

145–56 *Father . . . twinkling*: Lancelot,
rejoicing with heavy irony in his
success, takes his father upstage
towards Shylock's door, while
Bassanio and Leonardo confer
downstage.

147–8 *table . . . fortune*: Lancelot
pretends to read his fortune in the
lines of his hand—which would be
laid on the Bible to swear an oath.

148 *Go to*: come along (an expression of
exasperation).

149 *simple . . . life*: straightforward lifeline
(ironic).
small trifle: trivial matter.

151 *simple coming-in*: only a (sexual)
beginning.

152 *'scape*: escape.

153 *'scapes*: adventures.

153–4 *if . . . woman*: Fortune is pictured
as being female and fickle.

154 *gear*: business.

155–6 *in the twinkling*: in the twinkling of
an eye.

158 *orderly bestow'd*: stowed neatly on
board.

159 *feast*: give a banquet for.

161 *endeavours*: efforts.

165 *have . . . you*: want to ask a favour.
You . . . it: it's yours.

167 *you . . . thee*: Bassanio drops into the
familiar form of address for his
admonishment.

168 *rude*: uncouth, outspoken.

169 *Parts*: qualities.
become thee: suit you.

171 *show*: appear.
172 *Something too liberal*: rather too free-
and-easy.
pain: care.
173 *allay*: moderate.
modesty: decorum.
174 *skipping*: boisterous, effervescent.
175 *misconster'd*: misconstrued,
misinterpreted.

177 *sober habit*: a) decent costume;
b) restrained behaviour.
178 *but*: only.

180 *saying*: being said.
hood: cover; Elizabethan men kept
their hats on indoors, even for meals.
182 *Use . . . civility*: maintain all forms of
good manners.
183 *one . . . ostent*: someone who is
thoroughly accustomed to showing a
serious appearance.
184 *grandam*: grandmother.
185 *bearing*: conduct.

186 *bar*: make an exception of.
gauge: measure, judge.

187 *were pity*: would be a pity.

189 *suit of mirth*: a) entertaining manner;
b) party dress.
190 *purpose*: intend.

170 And in such eyes as ours appear not faults;
But where thou art not known, why there they show
Something too liberal. Pray thee take pain
To allay with some cold drops of modesty
Thy skipping spirit, lest through thy wild behaviour
175 I be misconster'd in the place I go to,
And lose my hopes.

Gratiano
                    Signor Bassanio, hear me:
If I do not put on a sober habit,
Talk with respect, and swear but now and then,
Wear prayer books in my pocket, look demurely,
180 Nay more, while grace is saying, hood mine eyes
Thus with my hat, and sigh and say 'amen',
Use all the observance of civility
Like one well studied in a sad ostent
To please his grandam, never trust me more.

Bassanio
185 Well, we shall see your bearing.

Gratiano
Nay, but I bar tonight, you shall not gauge me
By what we do tonight.

Bassanio
                          No, that were pity.
I would entreat you rather to put on
Your boldest suit of mirth, for we have friends
190 That purpose merriment. But fare you well,
I have some business.

Gratiano
And I must to Lorenzo and the rest;
But we will visit you at supper time.   [*Exeunt*

Act 2 Scene 3
Lancelot says goodbye to Jessica, Shylock's daughter.

3 *taste*: feeling.

SCENE 3

Venice: outside Shylock's house. Enter Jessica *and* Lancelot *the Clown*

Jessica
I am sorry thou wilt leave my father so.
Our house is hell, and thou a merry devil
Didst rob it of some taste of tediousness.
But fare thee well: there is a ducat for thee.
5 And, Lancelot, soon at supper shalt thou see
Lorenzo, who is thy new master's guest;
Give him this letter, do it secretly.
And so farewell: I would not have my father
See me in talk with thee.
Lancelot

10 *Adieu*: goodbye (French); Lancelot's high-flown language contrasts with Jessica's simple words.
exhibit my tongue: a) inhibit me from speaking; b) express what I can't say in words.
12 *get*: get hold of, steal.
13 *something*: somewhat, rather.

10 Adieu; tears exhibit my tongue. Most beautiful pagan, most sweet Jew, if a Christian do not play the knave and get thee, I am much deceived. But adieu; these foolish drops do something drown my manly spirit. Adieu!
[*Exit*

15 *heinous*: monstrous, abominable.

Jessica
Farewell, good Lancelot.
15 Alack, what heinous sin is it in me
To be asham'd to be my father's child!
But though I am a daughter to his blood

18 *manners*: behaviour.
19 *keep promise*: keep your promise.

I am not to his manners. O Lorenzo,
If thou keep promise, I shall end this strife,
20 Become a Christian and thy loving wife.
[*Exit*

Act 2 Scene 4
Lorenzo is planning some late-night entertainment when Lancelot brings a letter from Jessica.

SCENE 4

Venice: outside Shylock's house. Enter Gratiano, Lorenzo, Salarino, *and* Solanio

1 *supper*: A meal eaten around 5.00 p.m.
2 *Disguise us*: Lorenzo is urging his friends to join him in a masque—which usually involved a spectacular entry with music and torches.

Lorenzo
Nay, we will slink away in supper time,
Disguise us at my lodging, and return
All in an hour.
Gratiano
We have not made good preparation.

5 *spoke us*: made arrangements for.

6 *quaintly order'd*: done with style.

9 *furnish us*: get ourselves ready.

10 *And*: if.
break up: unseal.
10–11 *seem to signify*: appear to indicate.
12 *hand*: handwriting.
12, 14 *fair hand*: a) elegant handwriting; b) beautiful hand.

15 *By your leave*: please excuse me (a phrase to excuse one's departure).

17 *sup*: come to supper.

19 *this*: i.e. a tip.

23 *provided of*: supplied with.

24 *straight*: immediately.

26 *some hour*: in about an hour.

Salarino
5 We have not spoke us yet of torchbearers.
Solanio
'Tis vile unless it may be quaintly order'd,
And better in my mind not undertook.
Lorenzo
'Tis now but four of clock; we have two hours
To furnish us.

Enter Lancelot *with a letter*

Friend Lancelot! What's the news?
Lancelot
10 And it shall please you to break up this, it shall seem to
signify.
Lorenzo
I know the hand; in faith, 'tis a fair hand,
And whiter than the paper it writ on
Is the fair hand that writ.
Gratiano
Love news, in faith!
Lancelot
15 By your leave, sir.
Lorenzo
Whither goest thou?
Lancelot
Marry, sir, to bid my old master the Jew to sup tonight
with my new master the Christian.
Lorenzo
Hold here, take this. Tell gentle Jessica
20 I will not fail her; speak it privately.   [*Exit* Lancelot
Go, gentlemen:
Will you prepare you for this masque tonight?
I am provided of a torchbearer.
Salarino
Ay marry, I'll be gone about it straight.
Solanio
25 And so will I.
Lorenzo
Meet me and Gratiano
At Gratiano's lodging some hour hence.

Salarino

'Tis good we do so.

[*Exeunt* Salarino *and* Solanio

Gratiano

Was not that letter from fair Jessica?

Lorenzo

I must needs tell thee all. She hath directed

30 How I shall take her from her father's house,

What gold and jewels she is furnish'd with,

What page's suit she hath in readiness.

If e'er the Jew her father come to heaven,

It will be for his gentle daughter's sake;

35 And never dare misfortune cross her foot,

Unless she do it under this excuse

That she is issue to a faithless Jew.

Come, go with me; peruse this as thou goest.

Fair Jessica shall be my torchbearer.   [*Exeunt*

Scene 5

Venice: outside Shylock's *house. Enter* Shylock *the
Jew and* Lancelot *his man that was, the Clown*

Shylock

Well, thou shalt see, thy eyes shall be thy judge,

The difference of old Shylock and Bassanio—

What, Jessica!—Thou shalt not gourmandize

As thou hast done with me—What, Jessica!—

5 And sleep, and snore, and rend apparel out.

Why, Jessica, I say!

Lancelot

                              Why, Jessica!

Shylock

Who bids thee call? I do not bid thee call.

Lancelot

Your worship was wont to tell me I could do nothing
without bidding.

---

29 *I . . . all*: I've just got to tell you
everything.
directed: instructed.
31 *furnish'd with*: in possession of.

34 *gentle*: Lorenzo seems to make a pun
with 'Gentile' (see *1*, 3, 173).
35 *foot*: path.
36 *she do it*: misfortune trips her up.
under: with.
37 *issue . . . Jew*: the child of a Jew
lacking Christian faith.
38 *peruse*: study.

Act 2 Scene 5
Shylock leaves Jessica in charge of his
house.

Os.d. *Clown*: i.e. the company
comedian—see *2, 2*, 0s.d. note.

2 *of*: between.

3 *gourmandize*: gorge yourself with food.

5 *rend . . . out*: wear out your clothes by
tearing them.

8 *wont*: accustomed.

11 *bid forth*: invited out.
12 *wherefore*: why.

15 *prodigal*: wastrel; see *1*, 1, 129 note.
16 *Look to*: take care of.
    right loath: very reluctant.
17 *There . . . rest*: something is being
    plotted to harm my peace of mind.
18 *tonight*: last night.
20 *reproach*: Lancelot means
    'approach'—but Shylock takes his
    word, not his meaning.
23–6 *it . . . afternoon*: Lancelot mocks
    Shylock's interpretation of his dream;
    'Black Monday' = Easter Monday, and
    'Ash Wednesday' is the first day of
    Lent (40 days *before* Easter).
29 *wry-neck'd fife*: a small pipe played
    sideways, giving the musician a
    twisted ('wry') neck.
30 *casements*: windows.
32 *with . . . faces*: wearing painted
    masks.
34 *shallow foppery*: frivolity.
35 *Jacob's staff*: Jacob, Shylock's hero
    (see *1*, 3, 66–83), had only one staff
    when he crossed the river Jordan, yet
    he returned a rich man (Genesis
    32:10).
36 *forth*: away from home.

Enter Jessica

Jessica
10 Call you? What is your will?
    Shylock
    I am bid forth to supper, Jessica.
    There are my keys. But wherefore should I go?
    I am not bid for love, they flatter me;
    But yet I'll go in hate, to feed upon
15 The prodigal Christian. Jessica my girl,
    Look to my house. I am right loath to go;
    There is some ill a-brewing towards my rest,
    For I did dream of money bags tonight.
    Lancelot
    I beseech you, sir, go; my young master doth expect
20 your reproach.
    Shylock
    So do I his.
    Lancelot
    And they have conspired together—I will not say you
    shall see a masque; but if you do, then it was not for
    nothing that my nose fell a-bleeding on Black Monday
25 last, at six a clock i'the morning, falling out that year on
    Ash Wednesday was four year in th'afternoon.
    Shylock
    What, are there masques? Hear you me, Jessica,
    Lock up my doors, and when you hear the drum
    And the vile squealing of the wry-neck'd fife,
30 Clamber not you up to the casements then
    Nor thrust your head into the public street
    To gaze on Christian fools with varnish'd faces;
    But stop my house's ears—I mean my casements—
    Let not the sound of shallow foppery enter
35 My sober house. By Jacob's staff I swear
    I have no mind of feasting forth tonight:
    But I will go. Go you before me, sirrah;
    Say I will come.
    Lancelot
                    I will go before, sir.
    [*Aside to* Jessica] Mistress, look out at window for all
      this:

41 *worth . . . eye*: The expression
    (= something very valuable) was
    proverbial; 'Jewès' is an old inflected
    genitive (= Jew's).

42 *Hagar's offspring*: Abraham rejected
    Hagar and her son (his child), who
    were driven into the wilderness to live
    as outcasts (Genesis 21:9–21).

44 *patch*: fool.

45 *profit*: learning his job.

46 *wildcat*: a nocturnal animal which
    rests by day.
    Drones . . . me: non-working bees do
    not live in my beehive.

48–9 *waste . . . purse*: squander the
    money he has borrowed.

52 *Fast . . . find*: keep what you've got,
    and you'll soon get more.

54 *cross'd*: thwarted.

40 There will come a Christian by
With be worth a Jewès eye.   [*Exit*
     Shylock
What says that fool of Hagar's offspring, ha?
     Jessica
His words were 'Farewell, mistress', nothing else.
     Shylock
The patch is kind enough, but a huge feeder,
45 Snail-slow in profit, and he sleeps by day
More than the wildcat. Drones hive not with me,
Therefore I part with him, and part with him
To one that I would have him help to waste
His borrow'd purse. Well, Jessica, go in;
50 Perhaps I will return immediately.
Do as I bid you, shut doors after you.
Fast bind, fast find:
A proverb never stale in thrifty mind.   [*Exit*
     Jessica
Farewell, and if my fortune be not cross'd,
55 I have a father, you a daughter, lost.   [*Exit*

Act 2 Scene 6
Lorenzo and his friends rescue Jessica from
her father's house.

0s.d. *masquers*: Fantastic costumes,
    grotesque masks, and torches help to
    create the Carnival atmosphere that
    Shylock feared.

1 *penthouse*: projecting upper storey of
    building; Gratiano may indicate the
    balcony above the stage doors, or the
    stage roof.

5 *lovers . . . clock*: lovers always come
    before their time (a near-proverbial
    saying).

6 *Venus' pigeons*: doves drawing Venus's
    chariot.

7 *seal . . . made*: make sure of new
    engagements.

7–8 *than . . . unforfeited*: than they
    usually do in keeping marriage vows
    ('obliged faith') unbroken.

8 *obliged*: obligèd.

9 *ever holds*: is always true.

Scene 6

Venice: outside Shylock's *house. Enter the masquers,*
Gratiano *and* Salarino

     Gratiano
This is the penthouse under which Lorenzo
Desir'd us to make stand.
     Salarino
His hour is almost past.
     Gratiano
And it is marvel he outdwells his hour,
5 For lovers ever run before the clock.
     Salarino
O, ten times faster Venus' pigeons fly
To seal love's bonds new made than they are wont
To keep obliged faith unforfeited!
     Gratiano
That ever holds: who riseth from a feast
10 With that keen appetite that he sits down?

11 *untread*: retrace.
12 *measures*: steps, paces (in a riding-school display of dressage).
   unbated fire: undiminished energy.
14 *chased*: chasèd.
15 *younger*: younger son.
16 *scarfed bark*: scarfèd; ship with all flags flying.
17 *embraced*: embracèd.
   strumpet: unfaithful (like a prostitute).
18 *the prodigal*: The Prodigal Son wasted his inheritance on prostitutes and riotous living (see *1, 1, 129*).
19 *over-weather'd ribs*: weather-beaten timbers.
20 *rent*: torn.

22 *long abode*: staying away so long.

26 *father*: father-in-law; Lorenzo is sarcastic.

36 *exchange*: change into male clothing.

Where is the horse that doth untread again
His tedious measures with the unbated fire
That he did pace them first? All things that are
Are with more spirit chased than enjoy'd.
15 How like a younger or a prodigal
The scarfed bark puts from her native bay,
Hugg'd and embraced by the strumpet wind!
How like the prodigal doth she return
With overweather'd ribs and ragged sails,
20 Lean, rent, and beggar'd by the strumpet wind!

Enter Lorenzo

Salarino
Here comes Lorenzo; more of this hereafter.
Lorenzo
Sweet friends, your patience for my long abode.
Not I but my affairs have made you wait.
When you shall please to play the thieves for wives,
25 I'll watch as long for you then. Approach—
Here dwells my father Jew. Ho! Who's within?

Enter Jessica *above, in boy's clothes*

Jessica
Who are you? Tell me, for more certainty,
Albeit I'll swear that I do know your tongue.
Lorenzo
Lorenzo, and thy love.
Jessica
30 Lorenzo certain, and my love indeed,
For who love I so much? And now who knows
But you, Lorenzo, whether I am yours?
Lorenzo
Heaven and thy thoughts are witness that thou art.
Jessica
Here, catch this casket, it is worth the pains.
35 I am glad 'tis night, you do not look on me,
For I am much asham'd of my exchange.
But love is blind, and lovers cannot see
The pretty follies that themselves commit;

40 *transformed*: transformèd.

43 *good sooth*: goodness knows.
   light: a) apparent; b) immodest.
44 *'tis . . . discovery*: the torchbearer's
   job is to show light on things.
45 *obscur'd*: concealed.

46 *garnish*: costume.

48 *close*: secretive.
   doth . . . runaway: is speeding by.
49 *stay'd*: waited.

50 *make fast*: lock up.
   gild myself: provide myself with
   (more) gold.
51 *straight*: immediately.

52 *by my hood*: upon my word.
   gentle: a) well-bred girl; b) Gentile.

53 *Beshrew me*: damn me (a mild oath,
   added for emphasis).
   heartily: with all my heart.
55 *be true*: see truly.

58 *Shall . . . soul*: she will always have a
   place in my faithful heart.
   placed: placèd.

59 *gentleman*: Lorenzo laughingly
   addresses Jessica in her page's
   costume.

For if they could, Cupid himself would blush
40 To see me thus transformed to a boy.
        Lorenzo
Descend, for you must be my torchbearer.
        Jessica
What, must I hold a candle to my shames?
They in themselves, good sooth, are too too light.
Why, 'tis an office of discovery, love,
45 And I should be obscur'd.
        Lorenzo
                                So are you, sweet,
Even in the lovely garnish of a boy.
But come at once,
For the close night doth play the runaway,
And we are stay'd for at Bassanio's feast.
        Jessica
50 I will make fast the doors, and gild myself
With some moe ducats, and be with you straight.
                                [*Exit* Jessica *above*
        Gratiano
Now by my hood, a gentle and no Jew!
        Lorenzo
Beshrew me but I love her heartily.
For she is wise, if I can judge of her,
55 And fair she is, if that mine eyes be true,
And true she is, as she hath prov'd herself:
And therefore like herself, wise, fair, and true,
Shall she be placed in my constant soul.

        Enter Jessica

What, art thou come? On, gentleman, away!
60 Our masquing mates by this time for us stay.
                                [*Exit with* Jessica

        Enter Antonio

        Antonio
Who's there?
        Gratiano
Signor Antonio?

'Some god direct my judgement!' (2, 7, 13). Sinéad Cusack as Portia and Terry Wood as Morocco, Royal Shakespeare Company, 1981.

Antonio

Fie, fie, Gratiano, where are all the rest?

'Tis nine a clock, our friends all stay for you.

65 No masque tonight: the wind is come about,

Bassanio presently will go aboard.

I have sent twenty out to seek for you.

Gratiano

I am glad on't; I desire no more delight

Than to be under sail and gone tonight.   [*Exeunt*

65 *is come about*: has changed direction.

66 *presently*: immediately.

69 *to . . . sail*: to sail away.

SCENE 7

Belmont: Portia's house. Enter Portia *with the* Prince of Morocco *and both their trains*

Portia

Go, draw aside the curtains and discover

The several caskets to this noble prince.

Now make your choice.

Morocco

This first of gold, who this inscription bears,

5 'Who chooseth me, shall gain what many men desire.'

The second silver, which this promise carries,

'Who chooseth me, shall get as much as he deserves.'

This third dull lead, with warning all as blunt,

'Who chooseth me, must give and hazard all he hath.'

10 How shall I know if I do choose the right?

Portia

The one of them contains my picture, prince.

If you choose that, then I am yours withal.

Morocco

Some god direct my judgement! Let me see:

I will survey th'inscriptions back again.

15 What says this leaden casket?

'Who chooseth me, must give and hazard all he hath.'

Must give—for what? For lead? Hazard for lead!

This casket threatens: men that hazard all

Do it in hope of fair advantages.

20 A golden mind stoops not to shows of dross;

I'll then nor give nor hazard aught for lead.

What says the silver with her virgin hue?

Act 2 Scene 7
The Prince of Morocco examines the caskets and makes his choice.

1 *discover*: reveal.

2 *several*: different.

8 *as blunt*: as plain as the metal.

9 *hazard*: risk.

12 *withal*: with the casket.

14 *back again*: in reverse order.

19 *fair advantages*: good returns.

20 *dross*: rubbish, impure metal.

21 *nor . . . nor*: neither . . . nor.

25 *even*: impartial.
26 *rated*: judged.
    estimation: reputation.

29 *afear'd . . . deserving*: unsure what I
    deserve.
30 *disabling*: belittling.

36 *grav'd*: engraved.

40 *mortal breathing*: living.
41 *Hyrcanian deserts*: The classical name
    for a savage region south of the
    Caspian Sea.
    vasty wilds: immense wildernesses.
42 *throughfares*: main roads.
44 *The watery kingdom*: Neptune's realm,
    the ocean.
44–5 *whose . . . heaven*: whose waves
    surge up to the sky.
45 *bar*: obstacle.
46 *spirits*: men of courage.
49 *like*: likely.
50–1 *it were . . . cerecloth*: lead would be
    too coarse to enfold the shroud.
51 *obscure*: dark; the emphasis is on the
    first syllable.
52 *immur'd*: walled in.
53 *ten . . . gold*: of ten times less value
    than pure ('tried') gold.
54–5 *Never . . . gold*: jewels as precious
    as Portia are never set in anything but
    gold.
56 *A coin . . . angel*: The coin, called an
    'angel', depicted the archangel
    Michael.
57 *Stamped*: stampèd.
    insculp'd upon: engraved.

61 *form*: picture.

'Who chooseth me, shall get as much as he deserves.'
As much as he deserves—pause there, Morocco,
25 And weigh thy value with an even hand.
If thou be'st rated by thy estimation
Thou dost deserve enough; and yet enough
May not extend so far as to the lady;
And yet to be afear'd of my deserving
30 Were but a weak disabling of myself.
As much as I deserve: why, that's the lady.
I do in birth deserve her, and in fortunes,
In graces, and in qualities of breeding:
But more than these, in love I do deserve.
35 What if I stray'd no farther, but chose here?
Let's see once more this saying grav'd in gold:
'Who chooseth me, shall gain what many men desire.'
Why, that's the lady; all the world desires her.
From the four corners of the earth they come
40 To kiss this shrine, this mortal breathing saint.
The Hyrcanian deserts and the vasty wilds
Of wide Arabia are as throughfares now
For princes to come view fair Portia.
The watery kingdom, whose ambitious head
45 Spits in the face of heaven, is no bar
To stop the foreign spirits, but they come
As o'er a brook to see fair Portia.
One of these three contains her heavenly picture.
Is't like that lead contains her? 'Twere damnation
50 To think so base a thought; it were too gross
To rib her cerecloth in the obscure grave.
Or shall I think in silver she's immur'd,
Being ten times undervalu'd to tried gold?
O sinful thought! Never so rich a gem
55 Was set in worse than gold. They have in England
A coin that bears the figure of an angel
Stamped in gold; but that's insculp'd upon:
But here an angel in a golden bed
Lies all within. Deliver me the key:
60 Here do I choose, and thrive I as I may.
    Portia
There take it, prince, and if my form lie there,
Then I am yours.

Morocco unlocks the gold casket

Morocco

          O hell! What have we here?
A carrion death, within whose empty eye
There is a written scroll. I'll read the writing.
65   'All that glisters is not gold;
  Often have you heard that told.
  Many a man his life hath sold
  But my outside to behold.
  Gilded tombs do worms infold.
70   Had you been as wise as bold,
  Young in limbs, in judgement old,
  Your answer had not been inscroll'd.
  Fare you well, your suit is cold.'
Cold indeed, and labour lost;
75 Then farewell heat, and welcome frost.
Portia, adieu; I have too griev'd a heart
To take a tedious leave: thus losers part.

            [*Exit* Morocco *with his train*

Portia

A gentle riddance! Draw the curtains, go.
Let all of his complexion choose me so.   [*Exeunt*

A flourish of cornets

63 *A carrion death*: a death's-head, a skull.

65 *glisters*: glitters.
72 *Your . . . inscroll'd*: you would not have got the answer on this scroll.
73 *your . . . cold*: your hopes are dead.

79 *of his complexion*: like him.

Act 2 Scene 8
Salarino and Solanio gossip about the news: Lorenzo is missing, Shylock has been robbed, and Antonio is in trouble.

1 *under sail*: sail away.

4 *rais'd*: roused.

Scene 8

Venice: a street. Enter Salarino *and* Solanio

Salarino

Why, man, I saw Bassanio under sail,
With him is Gratiano gone along;
And in their ship I am sure Lorenzo is not.

Solanio

The villain Jew with outcries rais'd the duke,
5 Who went with him to search Bassanio's ship.

Salarino

He came too late, the ship was under sail.
But there the duke was given to understand

8 *gondola*: a flat-bottomed boat used on the canals of Venice.

10 *certified*: assured.

18 *sealed*: sealèd.

19 *double ducats*: worth double the value of ducats.

24 *his stones*: a) jewels; b) testicles.

25 *look . . . day*: be sure to pay his debt on the appointed day.

28 *reason'd*: spoke.

29 *the Narrow Seas*: the English Channel.

30 *miscarried*: miscarrièd; perished.

31 *fraught*: laden.

That in a gondola were seen together
Lorenzo and his amorous Jessica.
10 Besides, Antonio certified the duke
They were not with Bassanio in his ship.
    Solanio
I never heard a passion so confus'd,
So strange, outrageous, and so variable,
As the dog Jew did utter in the streets:
15 'My daughter! O my ducats! O my daughter!
Fled with a Christian! O my Christian ducats!
Justice! The law! My ducats and my daughter!
A sealed bag, two sealed bags of ducats,
Of double ducats, stolen from me by my daughter!
20 And jewels—two stones, two rich and precious stones,
Stolen by my daughter! Justice! Find the girl!
She hath the stones upon her and the ducats!'
    Salarino
Why, all the boys in Venice follow him,
Crying his stones, his daughter, and his ducats.
    Solanio
25 Let good Antonio look he keep his day,
Or he shall pay for this.
    Salarino
Marry, well remember'd:
I reason'd with a Frenchman yesterday
Who told me, in the Narrow Seas that part
30 The French and English, there miscarried
A vessel of our country richly fraught.
I thought upon Antonio when he told me,
And wish'd in silence that it were not his.

Solanio
You were best to tell Antonio what you hear.
35 Yet do not suddenly, for it may grieve him.
Salarino
A kinder gentleman treads not the earth.
I saw Bassanio and Antonio part:
Bassanio told him he would make some speed
Of his return: he answered, 'Do not so.
40 Slubber not business for my sake, Bassanio,
But stay the very riping of the time;
And for the Jew's bond which he hath of me,
Let it not enter in your mind of love.
Be merry, and employ your chiefest thoughts
45 To courtship, and such fair ostents of love
As shall conveniently become you there.'
And even there, his eye being big with tears,
Turning his face, he put his hand behind him,
And with affection wondrous sensible
50 He wrung Bassanio's hand, and so they parted.
Solanio
I think he only loves the world for him.
I pray thee let us go and find him out
And quicken his embraced heaviness
With some delight or other.
Salarino
                                                Do we so.   [*Exeunt*

SCENE 9

Belmont: Portia's house. *Enter* Nerissa *and a* Servitor

Nerissa
Quick, quick, I pray thee, draw the curtain straight.
The Prince of Arragon hath tane his oath,
And comes to his election presently.

A flourish of cornets. Enter the Prince of Arragon, *his train, and* Portia

Portia
Behold, there stand the caskets, noble prince.

---

40 *Slubber not business*: don't be hurried and careless with your affairs.
41 *stay . . . time*: wait until the time is exactly right.
42 *for*: as for.
43 *mind of love*: love-schemes.

45 *ostents*: demonstrations.
46 *conveniently become you*: make you appropriately attractive.
47 *even there*: just at that point.

49 *affection . . . sensible*: amazingly powerful emotion.

51 *he . . . him*: Bassanio is all he lives for.

53 *quicken . . . heaviness*: brighten up this misery that he's indulging in.
embraced: embracèd.

Act 2 Scene 9
Another suitor makes his choice—and Portia learns that Bassanio is coming to Belmont.

0s.d. *Servitor*: servingman.

1 *draw*: pull back.
straight: immediately.

3 *to his election*: to make his choice.

6 *solemniz'd*: performed.

9 *enjoin'd*: bound.
  observe: promise.
10 *unfold*: disclose.

14 *do . . . choice*: make an unlucky
   choice.

17 *hazard*: gamble.

18 *address'd me*: prepared myself (by
   taking the oath).
   Fortune: good luck.

24–5 *be . . . By*: refer to.
25 *show*: appearance.
26 *fond*: foolish.
27 *pries not*: doesn't look into.
   the martlet: the swift, or house-
   martin.
28 *Builds . . . weather*: builds its nest
   exposed to the weather.
29 *Even . . . casualty*: right in the power
   and path of destruction.
31 *jump*: go along with.
32 *rank me*: class myself.
36–7 *go . . . cozen*: try to cheat.
38 *Without . . . merit*: without the legal
   authorization ('stamp') of merit.
39 *wear*: hold; positions of rank and
   authority are usually indicated by the
   wearing of some badge or garment.
   undeserved: undeservèd.
40 *estates . . . offices*: estates of the
   realm (e.g. nobility), ranks within
   these estates (e.g. earls, barons), and
   official appointments (e.g. the
   chancellorship).
41 *deriv'd*: obtained.
42 *the wearer*: the bearer.

5 If you choose that wherein I am contain'd,
   Straight shall our nuptial rites be solemniz'd;
   But if you fail, without more speech, my lord,
   You must be gone from hence immediately.
       Arragon
   I am enjoin'd by oath to observe three things:
10 First, never to unfold to anyone
   Which casket 'twas I chose; next, if I fail
   Of the right casket, never in my life
   To woo a maid in way of marriage; lastly,
   If I do fail in fortune of my choice,
15 Immediately to leave you and be gone.
       Portia
   To these injunctions everyone doth swear
   That comes to hazard for my worthless self.
       Arragon
   And so have I address'd me. Fortune now
   To my heart's hope! Gold, silver, and base lead.
20 'Who chooseth me, must give and hazard all he hath.'
   You shall look fairer ere I give or hazard.
   What says the golden chest? Ha, let me see:
   'Who chooseth me, shall gain what many men desire.'
   What many men desire: that 'many' may be meant
25 By the fool multitude that choose by show,
   Not learning more than the fond eye doth teach,
   Which pries not to th'interior, but like the martlet
   Builds in the weather on the outward wall,
   Even in the force and road of casualty.
30 I will not choose what many men desire,
   Because I will not jump with common spirits,
   And rank me with the barbarous multitudes.
   Why then, to thee, thou silver treasure house:
   Tell me once more what title thou dost bear.
35 'Who chooseth me, shall get as much as he deserves.'
   And well said too, for who shall go about
   To cozen Fortune and be honourable
   Without the stamp of merit? Let none presume
   To wear an undeserved dignity.
40 O, that estates, degrees, and offices
   Were not deriv'd corruptly, and that clear honour
   Were purchas'd by the merit of the wearer!

43 *cover*: keep their hats on (instead of doffing them in respect to superiors).

45 *glean'd*: picked out.

47 *Pick'd . . . times*: sorted out from what the modern age rejects and spoils.
48 *new varnish'd*: a) polished up (like grains of corn); b) newly-painted (as a coat-of-arms).
50 *I will . . . desert*: I will claim to be deserving ('assume' = put on the ceremonial insignia of).

52 *Too . . . pause*: Arragon is speechless.
53 *blinking*: goggle-eyed.

54 *schedule*: written scroll.
60–1 *To . . . natures*: Portia cannot comment on the offence she has (unwittingly) given Arragon.
61 *opposed*: oppos*è*d.

62 *The . . . this*: this silver was tested seven times in the furnace.

64 *amiss*: wrongly.
65 *shadows kiss*: embrace illusions.

67 *iwis*: assuredly.
68 *Silver'd o'er*: covered in silver (with decorations, or with white hair).
69–70 *Take . . . head*: whatever wife you marry, you will always be a fool.
71 *sped*: finished.
72–3 *Still . . . here*: I shall appear an even bigger fool the longer I stay here.

How many then should cover that stand bare!
How many be commanded that command!
45 How much low peasantry would then be glean'd
From the true seed of honour, and how much honour
Pick'd from the chaff and ruin of the times
To be new varnish'd! Well, but to my choice.
'Who chooseth me, shall get as much as he deserves.'
50 I will assume desert. Give me a key for this,
And instantly unlock my fortunes here.

Arragon *unlocks the silver casket*

Portia
Too long a pause for that which you find there.
  Arragon
What's here? The portrait of a blinking idiot
Presenting me a schedule! I will read it.
55 How much unlike art thou to Portia!
How much unlike my hopes and my deservings.
'Who chooseth me, shall have as much as he deserves.'
Did I deserve no more than a fool's head?
Is that my prize? Are my deserts no better?
  Portia
60 To offend and judge are distinct offices,
And of opposed natures.
  Arragon
                      What is here?
[*He reads*] 'The fire seven times tried this;
    Seven times tried that judgement is
    That did never choose amiss.
65   Some there be that shadows kiss;
    Such have but a shadow's bliss.
    There be fools alive iwis
    Silver'd o'er, and so was this.
    Take what wife you will to bed,
70   I will ever be your head.
    So be gone, you are sped.'
Still more fool I shall appear
By the time I linger here.
With one fool's head I came to woo,
75 But I go away with two.

77 *wroth*: A possible spelling of either 'ruth' (= grief), or 'wrath'.

78 *singed*: burnt.

79 *deliberate*: reasoning, debating.

80 *They . . . lose*: their reasoning ('wit') gives them the wisdom to make the wrong choice.

81 *The . . . heresy*: the old proverb was no mistaken belief.

82 *wiving*: marrying.

84 *what . . . lord*: what do you want (Portia is ironic).

85 *alighted*: landed, dismounted.

87 *signify*: announce.

88 *sensible regrets*: tangible greetings (i.e. gifts).

89 *commends . . . breath*: compliments and polite speeches.

91 *likely*: a) promising; b) handsome.

92 *A day in April*: In England.

93 *costly*: rich (in flowers). *at hand*: near.

94 *forespurrer*: herald (who spurs his horse ahead of the main party).

95 *afear'd*: afraid.

96 *anon*: presently.

97 *highday wit*: well-dressed language.

99 *post*: messenger. *mannerly*: courteously.

100 *Bassanio . . . be*: O Lord Love, let it be Bassanio.

Sweet, adieu; I'll keep my oath,
Patiently to bear my wroth.

[*Exit* Arragon *with his train*

Portia
Thus hath the candle singed the moth.
O, these deliberate fools! When they do choose
80 They have the wisdom by their wit to lose.

Nerissa
The ancient saying is no heresy:
'Hanging and wiving goes by destiny.'

Portia
Come draw the curtain, Nerissa.

Enter a Messenger

Messenger
Where is my lady?

Portia
                                    Here. What would my lord?

Messenger
85 Madam, there is alighted at your gate
A young Venetian, one that comes before
To signify th'approaching of his lord,
From whom he bringeth sensible regrets:
To wit, besides commends and courteous breath,
90 Gifts of rich value. Yet I have not seen
So likely an ambassador of love.
A day in April never came so sweet
To show how costly summer was at hand
As this forespurrer comes before his lord.

Portia
95 No more I pray thee, I am half afear'd
Thou wilt say anon he is some kin to thee,
Thou spend'st such highday wit in praising him.
Come, come, Nerissa, for I long to see
Quick Cupid's post that comes so mannerly.

Nerissa
100 Bassanio, Lord Love, if thy will it be!   [*Exeunt*

SCENE 1

Venice: a street. Enter Solanio *and* Salarino

Solanio
Now, what news on the Rialto?
Salarino
Why, yet it lives there unchecked that Antonio hath a
ship of rich lading wrecked on the Narrow Seas; the
Goodwins I think they call the place—a very dangerous
5 flat, and fatal, where the carcasses of many a tall ship lie
buried, as they say, if my gossip Report be an honest
woman of her word.
Solanio
I would she were as lying a gossip in that as ever
knapped ginger or made her neighbours believe she
10 wept for the death of a third husband. But it is true,
without any slips of prolixity, or crossing the plain
highway of talk, that the good Antonio, the honest
Antonio—O that I had a title good enough to keep his
name company!—
Salarino
15 Come, the full stop.
Solanio
Ha, what sayest thou? Why, the end is, he hath lost a
ship.
Salarino
I would it might prove the end of his losses.
Solanio
Let me say 'amen' betimes, lest the devil cross my prayer,
20 for here he comes in the likeness of a Jew.

Enter Shylock

How now, Shylock, what news among the merchants?

---

2 *it lives*: the rumour persists.
  unchecked: without contradiction.
3 *lading*: loading, cargo.
  the Narrow Seas: the English Channel.
4 *the Goodwins*: The Goodwin Sands in
  the middle of the Channel are a major
  hazard for shipping.
5 *flat*: sandbank.
  tall: fine.
6 *my gossip Report*: my old friend
  Rumour ('gossip' = godmother).
8 *in that*: in that report.
9 *knapped*: munched; ginger (also
  associated with old women in *Measure
  for Measure*, *4*, 3, 7) is good for
  flatulence.
11–12 *without . . . talk*: without falling
  into garrulousness or deviating from a
  straightforward account; Solanio
  illustrates the fault he claims to avoid.

15 *Come . . . stop*: a) finish your
  sentence; b) rein in your horse (from a
  full gallop).

19 *betimes*: quickly.
  cross: a) frustrate; b) sign with a
  cross.

Shylock

You knew, none so well, none so well as you, of my daughter's flight.

Salarino

That's certain; I for my part knew the tailor that made 25 the wings she flew withal.

Solanio

And Shylock for his own part knew the bird was fledged, and then it is the complexion of them all to leave the dam.

Shylock

She is damned for it.

Salarino

30 That's certain—if the devil may be her judge.

Shylock

My own flesh and blood to rebel!

Solanio

Out upon it, old carrion! Rebels it at these years?

Shylock

I say my daughter is my flesh and my blood.

Salarino

There is more difference between thy flesh and hers 35 than between jet and ivory; more between your bloods than there is between red wine and Rhenish. But tell us, do you hear whether Antonio have had any loss at sea or no?

Shylock

There I have another bad match: a bankrupt, a prodigal, 40 who dare scarce show his head on the Rialto, a beggar that was used to come so smug upon the mart. Let him look to his bond. He was wont to call me usurer; let him look to his bond. He was wont to lend money for a Christian courtesy; let him look to his bond.

Salarino

45 Why, I am sure if he forfeit thou wilt not take his flesh. What's that good for?

Shylock

To bait fish withal; if it will feed nothing else, it will feed my revenge. He hath disgraced me, and hindered me half a million, laughed at my losses, mocked at my 50 gains, scorned my nation, thwarted my bargains, cooled

Glossary

25 *withal*: with.

27 *fledged*: had feathers.
complexion: nature, disposition.
28 *dam*: mother.

30 *the devil*: i.e. Shylock himself.

32 *Out . . . carrion*: get away with you, you dirty old man; Solanio pretends that Shylock is referring to his own body.

36 *Rhenish*: expensive white German wine.

39 *match*: bargain.

41 *smug*: pleased with himself.
mart: stock exchange.
42 *look to*: take care of.
wont: accustomed.
43–4 *for . . . courtesy*: out of Christian charity.

47 *bait*: use as a bait for.
48 *disgraced*: done me disfavour.
48–9 *hindered . . . million*: prevented me from making half a million ducats profit.
50 *bargains*: business deals.
cooled: alienated.

51 *heated*: enraged.

53 *dimensions*: bodily parts, limbs.
affections, passions: Elizabethan
psychology distinguished between
'affections' (= strong sensuous
responses of attraction or revulsion)
and 'passions' (= disturbances of the
mind).

61 *what . . . humility*: what is the
response of his Christian humility.
62 *sufferance*: forebearance (see
1, 3, 105).
64–5 *it . . . instruction*: unless something
serious prevents me, I will improve on
what you have taught me.

68 *up . . . him*: looking everywhere for
him.

69–70 *cannot be matched*: cannot be
found to equal these two.

76 *Frankfurt*: A great jewel fair was held
here annually.
76–7 *The . . . nation*: The Jews were
cursed and condemned to eternal
exile because they disobeyed God's
law (Daniel 9:11).

my friends, heated mine enemies—and what's his
reason? I am a Jew. Hath not a Jew eyes? Hath not a Jew
hands, organs, dimensions, senses, affections, passions?
Fed with the same food, hurt with the same weapons,
55 subject to the same diseases, healed by the same means,
warmed and cooled by the same winter and summer as
a Christian is? If you prick us, do we not bleed? If you
tickle us, do we not laugh? If you poison us, do we not
die? And if you wrong us, shall we not revenge? If we are
60 like you in the rest, we will resemble you in that. If a Jew
wrong a Christian, what is his humility? Revenge. If a
Christian wrong a Jew, what should his sufferance be by
Christian example? Why, revenge! The villainy you
teach me I will execute, and it shall go hard but I will
65 better the instruction.

Enter a Servingman *from* Antonio

Servingman
Gentlemen, my master Antonio is at his house, and
desires to speak with you both.
Salarino
We have been up and down to seek him.

Enter Tubal

Solanio
Here comes another of the tribe; a third cannot be
70 matched, unless the devil himself turn Jew.
[*Exeunt* Salarino *and* Solanio *with the* Servingman
Shylock
How now, Tubal, what news from Genoa? Hast thou
found my daughter?
Tubal
I often came where I did hear of her, but cannot find
her.
Shylock
75 Why there, there, there, there! A diamond gone cost me
two thousand ducats in Frankfurt! The curse never fell
upon our nation till now, I never felt it till now. Two
thousand ducats in that, and other precious, precious

80 *hearsed*: laid in her coffin.

82–3 *Why . . . loss*: Shylock's angry grief
makes him inarticulate.

85 *lights o'*: lands upon.

86 *but o'my breathing*: except those I
sigh.

91 *argosy*: trading vessel.
cast away: wrecked.

96 *one night*: in one night.

99 *at a sitting*: on a single occasion.

100 *divers*: several.
100–1 *in my company*: along with me.

102 *break*: go bankrupt.

105 *of*: from.

jewels! I would my daughter were dead at my foot, and
80 the jewels in her ear: would she were hearsed at my foot,
and the ducats in her coffin. No news of them, why so?
And I know not what's spent in the search. Why thou
loss upon loss—the thief gone with so much, and so
much to find the thief, and no satisfaction, no revenge,
85 nor no ill luck stirring but what lights o'my shoulders,
no sighs but o'my breathing, no tears but o'my
shedding!

Tubal

Yes, other men have ill luck too. Antonio as I heard in
Genoa—

Shylock

90 What, what, what? Ill luck, ill luck?

Tubal

—hath an argosy cast away coming from Tripolis.

Shylock

I thank God, I thank God. Is it true, is it true?

Tubal

I spoke with some of the sailors that escaped the wreck.

Shylock

I thank thee, good Tubal: good news, good news! Ha,
95 ha, heard in Genoa!

Tubal

Your daughter spent in Genoa, as I heard, one night
four score ducats.

Shylock

Thou stick'st a dagger in me; I shall never see my gold
again. Four score ducats at a sitting! Four score ducats!

Tubal

100 There came divers of Antonio's creditors in my
company to Venice that swear he cannot choose but
break.

Shylock

I am very glad of it. I'll plague him, I'll torture him. I am
glad of it.

Tubal

105 One of them showed me a ring that he had of your
daughter for a monkey.

107 *Out upon her*: A common expression
of impatience.
108 *had it of Leah*: it was a present from
Leah; Shylock's wife is presumably
dead.
110 *undone*: ruined.
111–12 *fee . . . officer*: hire a sheriff's
officer at my expense (to arrest
Antonio).
112 *bespeak . . . before*: order him to be
ready two weeks before the debt's
repayment is due.
114 *make . . . will*: drive whatever bargains
I like.
115 *synagogue*: The Jewish moneylenders
will confirm their dealings with an
oath.

Shylock

Out upon her! Thou torturest me, Tubal: it was my
turquoise, I had it of Leah when I was a bachelor. I
would not have given it for a wilderness of monkeys.

Tubal

110 But Antonio is certainly undone.

Shylock

Nay, that's true, that's very true. Go, Tubal, fee me an
officer, bespeak him a fortnight before. I will have the
heart of him if he forfeit, for were he out of Venice I can
make what merchandise I will. Go, Tubal, and meet me
115 at our synagogue, go, good Tubal, at our synagogue,
Tubal.   [*Exeunt*

Act 3 Scene 2
Bassanio makes his choice of caskets,
winning Portia for his wife. Nerissa agrees
to marry Gratiano, and both contracts are
sealed with a ring. Lorenzo and Jessica
arrive in Belmont, bringing a letter from
Antonio.

0s.d. *trains*: attendants.
1 *tarry*: delay.
2 *hazard*: take the risk.

5 *I would not*: I don't want to.

6 *Hate . . . quality*: hatred does not give
advice in this manner.

8 *a maiden . . . thought*: maidenly
modesty won't let me speak my
thoughts.
10 *venture for me*: try to win me.
11 *am forsworn*: have broken my vow.

12 *miss*: lose.

Scene 2

Belmont: Portia's *house. Enter* Bassanio, Portia,
Gratiano, Nerissa, *and all their trains*

Portia

I pray you tarry, pause a day or two
Before you hazard, for in choosing wrong
I lose your company; therefore forbear a while.
There's something tells me, but it is not love,
5 I would not lose you; and you know yourself
Hate counsels not in such a quality.
But lest you should not understand me well—
And yet a maiden hath no tongue but thought—
I would detain you here some month or two
10 Before you venture for me. I could teach you
How to choose right, but then I am forsworn.
So will I never be. So may you miss me;

13–14 *wish . . . forsworn*: wish I had
sinned and broken my vow.
14 *Beshrew*: a curse upon.
15 *o'erlook'd*: bewitched.

18–19 *these . . . rights*: these wicked
times bar owners from claiming what
belongs to them.
20 *Prove it so*: if it happens that I am lost
to you.
21 *Let . . . hell*: let Fortune go to hell for
depriving you of what is yours.
22 *peize*: weigh down, prolong.
23 *eche it*: stretch it out.
24 *stay . . . election*: hold you back from
making a choice.

25 *the rack*: an instrument of torture,
stretching out the victim's body (as
Portia is trying to stretch out the time)
until he confessed his treason.

28 *mistrust*: anxiety.
29 *fear . . . love*: afraid that I shall not be
able to have you as my wife.
30 *amity*: friendship.

33 *enforced*: enforcèd; compelled (by
torture).

36 *Had . . . confession*: would have been
my full confession.

38 *deliverance*: release.

42 *aloof*: at a distance, upstage.

But if you do, you'll make me wish a sin,
That I had been forsworn. Beshrew your eyes!
15 They have o'erlook'd me and divided me:
One half of me is yours, the other half yours—
Mine own, I would say: but if mine then yours,
And so all yours. O these naughty times
Puts bars between the owners and their rights!
20 And so though yours, not yours. Prove it so,
Let Fortune go to hell for it, not I.
I speak too long, but 'tis to peize the time,
To eche it, and to draw it out in length,
To stay you from election.
    Bassanio
                      Let me choose,
25 For as I am, I live upon the rack.
    Portia
Upon the rack, Bassanio? Then confess
What treason there is mingl'd with your love.
    Bassanio
None but that ugly treason of mistrust
Which makes me fear th'enjoying of my love.
30 There may as well be amity and life
'Tween snow and fire, as treason and my love.
    Portia
Ay, but I fear you speak upon the rack
Where men enforced do speak anything.
    Bassanio
Promise me life and I'll confess the truth.
    Portia
35 Well then, confess and live.
    Bassanio
                      'Confess and love'
Had been the very sum of my confession.
O happy torment, when my torturer
Doth teach me answers for deliverance!
But let me to my fortune and the caskets.
    Portia
40 Away then! I am lock'd in one of them:
If you do love me, you will find me out.
Nerissa and the rest, stand all aloof.
Let music sound while he doth make his choice;

44 *swan-like end*: It was an old belief
   that the mute swan sang once before
   its death.
45 *Fading*: dying, vanishing away.
46 *stand . . . proper*: fit more exactly.
46–7 *my eye . . . him*: I shall weep, and
   he will seem to drown in my tears.
49 *flourish*: trumpet fanfare.
50 *crowned*: crownèd.
51 *dulcet*: sweet.

54 *presence*: noble bearing.
55 *Alcides*: Hercules (grandson of Alceus)
   rescued a Trojan princess, Hesione,
   who was being sacrificed to a sea-
   monster.
56 *howling*: lamenting.
57 *I . . . sacrifice*: I represent the
   sacrificial victim.
58 *Dardanian wives*: Trojan women;
   Dardanus was the legendary founder
   of Troy.
59 *bleared visages*: blearèd; tear-stained
   faces.
60 *issue*: outcome.
61 *Live thou*: if you live.
62 *fray*: fighting.
62s.d. *comments . . . himself*: ponders
   silently over the caskets; the words of
   the song seem to articulate his
   thoughts.
63 *fancy*: attraction.
64 *Or . . . or*: either . . . or.
65 *nourished*: nourishèd.
67 *engend'red*: generated.

69 *in the cradle*: i.e. in its infancy.
70 *knell*: funeral bell.

73 *shows*: appearances.
   least themselves: not what they are.
74 *still*: continually.
76 *season'd . . . voice*: presented with
   eloquence (like rotten food disguised
   with spices).
78 *damned error*: damnèd; heresy, false
   belief.
   sober brow: solemn-faced person.

Then if he lose he makes a swan-like end,
45 Fading in music. That the comparison
May stand more proper, my eye shall be the stream
And watery deathbed for him. He may win,
And what is music then? Then music is
Even as the flourish when true subjects bow
50 To a new-crowned monarch. Such it is
As are those dulcet sounds in break of day,
That creep into the dreaming bridegroom's ear
And summon him to marriage. Now he goes
With no less presence, but with much more love,
55 Than young Alcides when he did redeem
The virgin tribute paid by howling Troy
To the sea-monster. I stand for sacrifice.
The rest aloof are the Dardanian wives,
With bleared visages come forth to view
60 The issue of th'exploit. Go, Hercules!
Live thou, I live. With much much more dismay
I view the fight than thou that mak'st the fray.

Here music. A song the whilst Bassanio *comments on
the caskets to himself*

Tell me where is fancy bred,
Or in the heart, or in the head?
65 How begot, how nourished?
   Reply, reply.
It is engend'red in the eye,
With gazing fed, and fancy dies
In the cradle where it lies.
70 Let us all ring fancy's knell.
I'll begin it—Ding, dong, bell.
All
   Ding, dong, bell.
Bassanio
So may the outward shows be least themselves:
The world is still deceiv'd with ornament.
75 In law, what plea so tainted and corrupt
But, being season'd with a gracious voice,
Obscures the show of evil? In religion,
What damned error but some sober brow

Will bless it and approve it with a text,
80 Hiding the grossness with fair ornament?
There is no vice so simple but assumes
Some mark of virtue on his outward parts.
How many cowards whose hearts are all as false
As stayers of sand, wear yet upon their chins
85 The beards of Hercules and frowning Mars,
Who inward search'd have livers white as milk,
And these assume but valour's excrement
To render them redoubted. Look on beauty,
And you shall see 'tis purchas'd by the weight,
90 Which therein works a miracle in nature,
Making them lightest that wear most of it.
So are those crisped snaky golden locks
Which maketh such wanton gambols with the wind
Upon supposed fairness, often known
95 To be the dowry of a second head,
The skull that bred them in the sepulchre.
Thus ornament is but the guiled shore
To a most dangerous sea; the beauteous scarf
Veiling an Indian beauty; in a word,
100 The seeming truth which cunning times put on
To entrap the wisest. Therefore thou gaudy gold,
Hard food for Midas, I will none of thee,
Nor none of thee, thou pale and common drudge
'Tween man and man. But thou, thou meagre lead
105 Which rather threaten'st than dost promise aught,
Thy paleness moves me more than eloquence:
And here choose I. Joy be the consequence!
   Portia
[*Aside*] How all the other passions fleet to air:
As doubtful thoughts, and rash-embrac'd despair,
110 And shudd'ring fear, and green-ey'd jealousy!
O love, be moderate, allay thy ecstasy,
In measure rain thy joy, scant this excess!
I feel too much thy blessing: make it less
For fear I surfeit.

Bassanio *opens the leaden casket*

Bassanio

115 *counterfeit*: picture.

116 *Move . . . eyes*: do these eyes move.
117 *riding . . . mine*: fixed on my eyes.
118 *sever'd*: parted.
119 *bar*: barrier (i.e. Portia's breath).
121 *painter . . . spider*: the painter has been like a spider.
123 *Faster*: more securely.
125 *power*: i.e. like the sun; Bassanio uses a conventional conceit.
126 *unfurnish'd*: without a mate.
    how far: by the extent to which.
127 *substance*: body.
    shadow: semblance.
128 *underprizing it*: failing to describe it adequately.
    so far: to the same extent.
130 *continent*: container.
132 *Chance . . . true*: may you have such good fortune and always choose as well.
136 *hold . . . bliss*: account your fortune happiness.
140 *by note*: with a bill of dues.
141 *prize*: match.
143 *universal*: general.

What find I here?
115 Fair Portia's counterfeit! What demi-god
Hath come so near creation? Move these eyes?
Or whether riding on the balls of mine
Seem they in motion? Here are sever'd lips
Parted with sugar breath; so sweet a bar
120 Should sunder such sweet friends. Here in her hairs
The painter plays the spider, and hath woven
A golden mesh t'entrap the hearts of men
Faster than gnats in cobwebs. But her eyes—
How could he see to do them? Having made one,
125 Methinks it should have power to steal both his
And leave itself unfurnish'd. Yet look how far
The substance of my praise doth wrong this shadow
In underprizing it, so far this shadow
Doth limp behind the substance. Here's the scroll,
130 The continent and summary of my fortune.
[*He reads*] 'You that choose not by the view
    Chance as fair, and choose as true.
    Since this fortune falls to you,
    Be content and seek no new.
135   If you be well pleas'd with this,
       And hold your fortune for your bliss,
       Turn to where your lady is,
       And claim her with a loving kiss.'
A gentle scroll! Fair lady, by your leave,
140 I come by note to give, and to receive.
Like one of two contending in a prize
That thinks he hath done well in people's eyes,
Hearing applause and universal shout,
Giddy in spirit, still gazing in a doubt
145 Whether those peals of praise be his or no—
So, thrice-fair lady, stand I even so,
As doubtful whether what I see be true,
Until confirm'd, sign'd, ratified by you.
    Portia
You see me, Lord Bassanio, where I stand,
150 Such as I am. Though for myself alone
I would not be ambitious in my wish

To wish myself much better, yet for you
I would be trebled twenty times myself,
A thousand times more fair, ten thousand times
155 More rich, that only to stand high in your account
I might in virtues, beauties, livings, friends,
Exceed account. But the full sum of me
Is sum of something: which to term in gross
Is an unlesson'd girl, unschool'd, unpractis'd;
160 Happy in this, she is not yet so old
But she may learn; happier than this,
She is not bred so dull but she can learn;
Happiest of all, is that her gentle spirit
Commits itself to yours to be directed
165 As from her lord, her governor, her king.
Myself, and what is mine, to you and yours
Is now converted. But now I was the lord
Of this fair mansion, master of my servants,
Queen o'er myself; and even now, but now,
170 This house, these servants, and this same myself
Are yours, my lord's. I give them with this ring,
Which when you part from, lose, or give away,
Let it presage the ruin of your love,
And be my vantage to exclaim on you.
 Bassanio
175 Madam, you have bereft me of all words.
Only my blood speaks to you in my veins,
And there is such confusion in my powers
As after some oration fairly spoke
By a beloved prince there doth appear
180 Among the buzzing, pleased multitude,
Where every something being blent together
Turns to a wild of nothing, save of joy
Express'd, and not express'd. But when this ring
Parts from this finger, then parts life from hence:
185 O then be bold to say Bassanio's dead!
 Nerissa
My lord and lady, it is now our time,
That have stood by and seen our wishes prosper,
To cry 'good joy'. Good joy, my lord and lady!

155 *That only*: only in order to.
156 *livings*: material possessions.
157 *account*: estimation.
158 *to . . . gross*: in gross terms.
159 *unpractis'd*: inexperienced.
160 *Happy*: fortunate.

162 *bred so dull*: born so stupid.

166–7 *Myself . . . converted*: I, and everything I possess, have now become your property.
167 *but now*: just a moment ago.
174 *vantage*: opportunity.
exclaim on: denounce.

175 *bereft me of*: stolen from me.
176 *my blood speaks*: Bassanio blushes.
177 *powers*: faculties.
178–83 *As . . . express'd*: Bassanio compares his mixed feelings to a happy mob of citizens after a well-delivered speech from their popular ruler.
179 *beloved*: belovèd.
180 *buzzing*: murmuring.
pleased: pleasèd.
181 *something*: little thing.
blent: blended, mixed.
182 *wild of nothing*: indistinguishable wilderness.
save: except.

190–1 *I wish . . . me*: I hope you will have all the joy you wish for yourselves, because I am sure you will not wish any of my joy away from me.
192 *solemnize*: formally celebrate.

194 *Even*: just.

195 *so*: provided that.

198 *maid*: lady-in-waiting.
199–200 *for . . . you*: I wasted no more spare time ('intermission') than you.
201 *stood*: depended.
202 *as . . . falls*: as it happens.
203 *until . . . again*: so hard that I was sweating.
204–5 *swearing . . . love*: making vows of love until the roof of my mouth was dry.
205 *if promise last*: if she keeps the promise; Gratiano puns on two senses of a word (also in line 211).
206 *of*: from.

209 *so . . . withal*: provided that you are pleased with it.

210 *mean good faith*: have good intentions.

211 *'faith*: upon my faith.

213–14 *We'll . . . ducats*: we'll wager a thousand ducats on who has the first son.

215 *stake down*: money for the bet laid on the table; Gratiano takes the slang sense 'with a limp penis'.
216 *infidel*: Gratiano refers to Jessica's Jewishness.

Gratiano
My lord Bassanio, and my gentle lady,
190 I wish you all the joy that you can wish;
For I am sure you can wish none from me.
And when your honours mean to solemnize
The bargain of your faith, I do beseech you
Even at that time I may be married too.
Bassanio
195 With all my heart, so thou canst get a wife.
Gratiano
I thank your lordship, you have got me one.
My eyes, my lord, can look as swift as yours:
You saw the mistress, I beheld the maid.
You lov'd, I lov'd; for intermission
200 No more pertains to me, my lord, than you.
Your fortune stood upon the caskets there,
And so did mine too as the matter falls.
For wooing here until I sweat again,
And swearing till my very roof was dry
205 With oaths of love, at last—if promise last—
I got a promise of this fair one here
To have her love, provided that your fortune
Achiev'd her mistress.
Portia
                                  Is this true, Nerissa?
Nerissa
Madam, it is, so you stand pleas'd withal.
Bassanio
210 And do you, Gratiano, mean good faith?
Gratiano
Yes 'faith, my lord.
Bassanio
Our feast shall be much honour'd in your marriage.
Gratiano
We'll play with them the first boy for a thousand ducats.
Nerissa
What, and stake down?
Gratiano
215 No, we shall ne'er win at that sport and stake down.
But who comes here? Lorenzo and his infidel!
What, and my old Venetian friend Salerio!

Enter Lorenzo, Jessica, *and* Salerio, *a messenger from Venice*

Bassanio
Lorenzo and Salerio, welcome hither—
If that the youth of my new interest here
220 Have power to bid you welcome. By your leave
I bid my very friends and countrymen,
Sweet Portia, welcome.

Portia
                              So do I, my lord.
They are entirely welcome.

Lorenzo
I thank your honour. For my part, my lord,
225 My purpose was not to have seen you here,
But meeting with Salerio by the way
He did entreat me past all saying nay
To come with him along.

Salerio
                              I did, my lord,
And I have reason for it. [*Giving letter*] Signor Antonio
230 Commends him to you.

Bassanio
                              Ere I ope his letter,
I pray you tell me how my good friend doth.

Salerio
Not sick, my lord, unless it be in mind,
Nor well, unless in mind: his letter there
Will show you his estate.

Bassanio *opens the letter*

Gratiano
235 Nerissa, cheer yond stranger, bid her welcome.
Your hand, Salerio; what's the news from Venice?
How doth that royal merchant, good Antonio?
I know he will be glad of our success;
We are the Jasons, we have won the fleece.

Salerio
240 I would you had won the fleece that he hath lost.

219–20 *If . . . welcome*: if my very new position here gives me the right to welcome you.
221 *very*: true.

223 *entirely*: heartily.

225 *My purpose was not*: I did not intend.
226 *by the way*: by chance.
227 *past . . . nay*: and would not let me refuse.

230 *Commends him*: sends his greetings.

233 *in mind*: in fortitude.
234 *estate*: condition.

235 *cheer*: welcome.
   yond: yonder.

237 *royal*: prince among merchants.

239 *Jasons*: See note on *1*, 1, 170.

240 *fleece*: Salerio puns on 'fleets'.

Portia

There are some shrewd contents in yond same paper
That steals the colour from Bassanio's cheek:
Some dear friend dead, else nothing in the world
Could turn so much the constitution

245 Of any constant man. What, worse and worse?
With leave, Bassanio, I am half yourself
And I must freely have the half of anything
That this same paper brings you.

Bassanio

                            O sweet Portia,
Here are a few of the unpleasant'st words

250 That ever blotted paper. Gentle lady,
When I did first impart my love to you,
I freely told you all the wealth I had
Ran in my veins: I was a gentleman.
And then I told you true; and yet, dear lady,

255 Rating myself at nothing, you shall see
How much I was a braggart. When I told you
My state was nothing, I should then have told you
That I was worse than nothing; for indeed
I have engag'd myself to a dear friend,

260 Engag'd my friend to his mere enemy,
To feed my means. Here is a letter, lady,
The paper as the body of my friend,
And every word in it a gaping wound
Issuing lifeblood. But is it true, Salerio?

265 Hath all his ventures failed? What, not one hit?
From Tripolis, from Mexico, and England,
From Lisbon, Barbary, and India,
And not one vessel 'scape the dreadful touch
Of merchant-marring rocks?

Salerio

                              Not one, my lord.

270 Besides, it should appear that if he had
The present money to discharge the Jew,
He would not take it. Never did I know
A creature that did bear the shape of man
So keen and greedy to confound a man.

275 He plies the duke at morning and at night,

---

241 *shrewd*: bitter.

244 *constitution*: complexion.
245 *constant*: normal.
246 *With leave*: excuse me.

250 *blotted paper*: spoiled a paper with ink.

252 *freely*: honestly.
253 *Ran in my veins*: was in my blood.

255 *Rating*: valuing.
256 *was a braggart*: boasted.

259 *engag'd*: bound.
260 *mere*: absolute.
261 *To feed my means*: to get the money I needed.
262 *as*: is like.

264 *Issuing lifeblood*: from which his lifeblood pours.
265 *ventures*: speculations.
   hit: succeeded.

269 *merchant-marring rocks*: rocks that ruin merchants.

271 *present*: ready.
   discharge: pay his debt to.

275 *plies*: urges his case on.

276 *impeach . . . state*: discredit the integrity of Venetian law.

278 *magnificoes*: noblemen.

279 *port*: eminence.
persuaded: argued.
280 *drive him from*: persuade him to give up.
envious plea: malicious claim.

283 *his countrymen*: fellow Jews.

287 *deny not*: do not prevent it.
288 *hard*: badly.

291 *best condition'd*: most good-natured.
292 *courtesies*: acts of kindness.
293 *The ancient Roman honour*: i.e. loyalty to friends and country.

297 *deface*: cancel.

301 *call me wife*: make me your wife.

309 *shall hence*: must go away from here.

And doth impeach the freedom of the state
If they deny him justice. Twenty merchants,
The duke himself, and the magnificoes
Of greatest port have all persuaded with him,
280 But none can drive him from the envious plea
Of forfeiture, of justice, and his bond.
    Jessica
When I was with him, I have heard him swear
To Tubal and to Chus, his countrymen,
That he would rather have Antonio's flesh
285 Than twenty times the value of the sum
That he did owe him; and I know, my lord,
If law, authority, and power deny not
It will go hard with poor Antonio.
    Portia
Is it your dear friend that is thus in trouble?
    Bassanio
290 The dearest friend to me, the kindest man,
The best condition'd and unwearied spirit
In doing courtesies; and one in whom
The ancient Roman honour more appears
Than any that draws breath in Italy.
    Portia
295 What sums owes he the Jew?
    Bassanio
For me, three thousand ducats.
    Portia
                         What, no more?
Pay him six thousand, and deface the bond.
Double six thousand, and then treble that,
Before a friend of this description
300 Shall lose a hair through Bassanio's fault.
First go with me to church, and call me wife,
And then away to Venice to your friend!
For never shall you lie by Portia's side
With an unquiet soul. You shall have gold
305 To pay the petty debt twenty times over.
When it is paid, bring your true friend along.
My maid Nerissa and myself meantime
Will live as maids and widows. Come away,
For you shall hence upon your wedding day.

310 *cheer*: face.
311 *dear bought*: expensively purchased.

313 *miscarried*: been lost.

316 *cleared*: cancelled.
317 *but*: only.
318 *use your pleasure*: do as you please.

320 *Dispatch*: quickly finish.

321 *good leave*: kind permission.

323–4 *No . . . twain*: no bed will be accused of holding me back, and no rest shall come between the two of us.

310 Bid your friends welcome, show a merry cheer;
Since you are dear bought, I will love you dear.
But let me hear the letter of your friend.

Bassanio
[*Reads*] 'Sweet Bassanio, my ships have all miscarried, my creditors grow cruel, my estate is very low; my bond
315 to the Jew is forfeit, and since in paying it, it is impossible I should live, all debts are cleared between you and I if I might but see you at my death. Notwithstanding, use your pleasure; if your love do not persuade you to come, let not my letter.'

Portia
320 O love! Dispatch all business and be gone.

Bassanio
Since I have your good leave to go away,
I will make haste. But till I come again
No bed shall e'er be guilty of my stay
Nor rest be interposer 'twixt us twain.   [*Exeunt*

Act 3 Scene 3
Antonio has been arrested and Shylock threatens him.

1 *look to him*: guard him carefully.
2 *gratis*: free of interest.

4 *speak not*: don't argue.
5 *my bond*: Shylock emphasizes the legality of his claim.

SCENE 3

Venice: a street. Enter Shylock *the Jew, and* Solanio, *and* Antonio, *and the* Jailer

Shylock
Jailer, look to him. Tell not me of mercy.
This is the fool that lent out money gratis.
Jailer, look to him.

Antonio
                    Hear me yet, good Shylock—

Shylock
I'll have my bond, speak not against my bond;
5 I have sworn an oath that I will have my bond.

8–10 *I . . . request*: It would appear that Antonio is being given some unusual privileges.

9 *naughty*: worthless.
fond: foolish.

10 *abroad*: out of the prison.

14 *dull-eyed*: stupid.
16 *intercessors*: pleaders.
18 *impenetrable*: hard-hearted.
19 *kept with*: lived among.
20 *bootless*: unsuccessful.

22 *deliver'd*: rescued.
forfeitures: actions for breach of contract (like that which Antonio now endures).
23 *made moan*: complained.

25 *grant*: allow.

27 *commodity*: privilege.
strangers: foreigners.

29 *impeach*: discredit.

31 *Consisteth of*: depends upon.
32 *bated me*: made me lose weight.

34 *bloody*: bloodthirsty.

Thou call'dst me dog before thou hadst a cause,
But since I am a dog, beware my fangs.
The duke shall grant me justice. I do wonder,
Thou naughty jailer, that thou art so fond
10 To come abroad with him at his request.
> **Antonio**
I pray thee hear me speak—
> **Shylock**
I'll have my bond; I will not hear thee speak;
I'll have my bond, and therefore speak no more.
I'll not be made a soft and dull-eyed fool,
15 To shake the head, relent, and sigh, and yield
To Christian intercessors. Follow not!
I'll have no speaking, I will have my bond.   [*Exit*
> **Solanio**
It is the most impenetrable cur
That ever kept with men.
> **Antonio**
                                        Let him alone.
20 I'll follow him no more with bootless prayers.
He seeks my life, his reason well I know:
I oft deliver'd from his forfeitures
Many that have at times made moan to me;
Therefore he hates me.
> **Solanio**
                                   I am sure the duke
25 Will never grant this forfeiture to hold.
> **Antonio**
The duke cannot deny the course of law;
For the commodity that strangers have
With us in Venice, if it be denied,
Will much impeach the justice of the state,
30 Since that the trade and profit of the city
Consisteth of all nations. Therefore go.
These griefs and losses have so bated me
That I shall hardly spare a pound of flesh
Tomorrow to my bloody creditor.
35 Well, jailer, on. Pray God Bassanio come
To see me pay his debt, and then I care not.   [*Exeunt*

Act 3 Scene 4
Portia and Nerissa plan a visit to Venice.

2 *conceit*: understanding.

3 *amity*: friendship.

5 *to whom*: i.e. Antonio.

7 *lover*: friend.

9 *customary . . . you*: your usual generosity must make you feel.

12 *waste*: spend.
13 *bear . . . love*: are joined equally together in love.
14 *needs*: of necessity.
like: similar.
15 *lineaments*: appearances.
17 *bosom lover*: intimate friend.

19 *bestow'd*: spent.
20 *semblance . . . soul*: likeness of the one I love.

22 *comes too near*: is too like.

25 *husbandry and manage*: careful management.

33 *deny*: refuse.
imposition: task.

SCENE 4

Belmont: Portia's house. Enter Portia, Nerissa, Lorenzo, Jessica, *and* Balthazar *a man of* Portia's

Lorenzo
Madam, although I speak it in your presence,
You have a noble and a true conceit
Of god-like amity, which appears most strongly
In bearing thus the absence of your lord.
5 But if you knew to whom you show this honour,
How true a gentleman you send relief,
How dear a lover of my lord your husband,
I know you would be prouder of the work
Than customary bounty can enforce you.
Portia
10 I never did repent for doing good,
Nor shall not now; for in companions
That do converse and waste the time together,
Whose souls do bear an equal yoke of love,
There must be needs a like proportion
15 Of lineaments, of manners, and of spirit;
Which makes me think that this Antonio,
Being the bosom lover of my lord,
Must needs be like my lord. If it be so,
How little is the cost I have bestow'd
20 In purchasing the semblance of my soul
From out the state of hellish cruelty!
This comes too near the praising of myself,
Therefore no more of it: hear other things.
Lorenzo, I commit into your hands
25 The husbandry and manage of my house
Until my lord's return; for mine own part
I have toward heaven breath'd a secret vow
To live in prayer and contemplation,
Only attended by Nerissa here,
30 Until her husband and my lord's return.
There is a monastery two miles off,
And there we will abide. I do desire you
Not to deny this imposition,

The which my love and some necessity
35 Now lays upon you.
       Lorenzo
                    Madam, with all my heart
I shall obey you in all fair commands.
       Portia
My people do already know my mind,
And will acknowledge you and Jessica
In place of Lord Bassanio and myself.
40 So fare you well till we shall meet again.
       Lorenzo
Fair thoughts and happy hours attend on you.
       Jessica
I wish your ladyship all heart's content.
       Portia
I thank you for your wish, and am well pleas'd
To wish it back on you: fare you well, Jessica.
                    [*Exeunt* Jessica *and* Lorenzo
45 Now, Balthazar—
As I have ever found thee honest-true,
So let me find thee still; take this same letter,
And use thou all th'endeavour of a man
In speed to Padua. See thou render this
50 Into my cousin's hand, Doctor Bellario;
And look, what notes and garments he doth give thee
Bring them, I pray thee, with imagin'd speed
Unto the traject, to the common ferry
Which trades to Venice. Waste no time in words
55 But get thee gone; I shall be there before thee.
       Balthazar
Madam, I go with all convenient speed.   [*Exit*
       Portia
Come on, Nerissa; I have work in hand
That you yet know not of. We'll see our husbands
Before they think of us.
       Nerissa
                    Shall they see us?
       Portia
60 They shall, Nerissa, but in such a habit
That they shall think we are accomplished

---

37 *people*: household.
   my mind: what I intend.
38 *acknowledge*: recognize your authority.

44 *wish . . . you*: with the same to you.

45 *Now, Balthazar*: The broken line allows for movement on the stage.
46 *ever*: always.
   honest-true: honest and trustworthy.
47 *So . . . still*: may I continue to find you so.
48 *all . . . man*: go as fast as a man can.
49 *render*: give.
51 *what*: whatever.
52 *imagin'd speed*: all the speed imaginable.
53 *the traject . . . ferry*: the ferry, the public transport.
54 *trades to*: communicates with.

56 *convenient*: appropriate.

57 *work in hand*: a plan in my mind.

59 *think of us*: expect to see us.

60 *habit*: costume.
61 *accomplished*: accomplishèd; equipped.

62 *that we lack*: i.e. male genitals.

63 *accoutred*: dressed up.

64 *prettier*: smarter.

66 *between . . . boy*: as though my voice were breaking.
67 *reed*: squeaky.
mincing: dainty, ladylike.
68 *'frays*: affrays, fights.
69 *bragging*: boastful.
quaint: elaborate.

72 *do withal*: help it.

75–6 *I have . . . twelvemonth*: it's more than a year since I left school (i.e. I'm a real man).
77 *raw*: crude.
jacks: fellows.

78 *turn to men*: change into men. Portia pretends to think that Nerissa means 'take men for lovers'.

80 *lewd interpreter*: someone with a dirty mind.
81 *device*: plan.

84 *measure*: travel.

Act 3 Scene 5
Lancelot teases Jessica.

1 *look you*: you see.
1–2 *the sins . . . children*: Lancelot quotes from the Second Commandment (Exodus 20:5).
2 *laid upon*: revenged upon.
2–3 *I fear you*: I fear for you.
3 *plain*: honest.
4 *agitation*: Lancelot means 'cogitation' (= considered opinion).
7 *bastard hope*: a) false hope; b) hope that you are a bastard.
neither: anyway.

With that we lack. I'll hold thee any wager,
When we are both accoutred like young men
I'll prove the prettier fellow of the two,
65 And wear my dagger with the braver grace,
And speak between the change of man and boy
With a reed voice, and turn two mincing steps
Into a manly stride; and speak of 'frays
Like a fine bragging youth; and tell quaint lies
70 How honourable ladies sought my love,
Which I denying, they fell sick and died—
I could not do withal. Then I'll repent,
And wish for all that that I had not kill'd them;
And twenty of these puny lies I'll tell,
75 That men shall swear I have discontinu'd school
Above a twelvemonth. I have within my mind
A thousand raw tricks of these bragging jacks,
Which I will practise.

Nerissa
               Why, shall we turn to men?

Portia
Fie, what a question's that,
80 If thou wert near a lewd interpreter!
But come, I'll tell thee all my whole device
When I am in my coach, which stays for us
At the park gate; and therefore haste away,
For we must measure twenty miles today.   *[Exeunt*

Scene 5

Belmont: Portia's garden. Enter Lancelot *the Clown and* Jessica

Lancelot
Yes truly, for look you, the sins of the father are to be
laid upon the children. Therefore I promise you I fear
you. I was always plain with you, and so now I speak my
agitation of the matter. Therefore be o'good cheer, for
5 truly I think you are damned. There is but one hope in
it that can do you any good, and that is but a kind of
bastard hope neither.

9 *got*: begot, fathered.

11 *so*: if that were the case.
12 *visited*: revenged.

14–15 *Scylla . . . Charybdis*: Monsters (a
rock-formation and a whirlpool)
threatening sailors of classical
mythology in the narrow straits
between Italy and Sicily.
15 *gone*: ruined, damned.
16 *saved . . . husband*: Jessica can quote
St Paul: 'the unbelieving wife is
sanctified by the husband'
(1 Corinthians 7:14).
18 *enow*: enough.
19 *e'en . . . another*: just enough to live
comfortably together.
21 *pork eaters*: Jews are forbidden to eat
pork.
21–2 *not . . . money*: soon not be able to
afford a rasher of fried bacon.

27–8 *are out*: have quarrelled.

30 *commonwealth*: general public.

33 *getting up*: swelling out.
Moor: Moorish woman (probably a
servant).

Jessica
And what hope is that, I pray thee?
Lancelot
Marry, you may partly hope that your father got you
10 not, that you are not the Jew's daughter.
Jessica
That were a kind of bastard hope indeed; so the sins of
my mother should be visited upon me.
Lancelot
Truly, then, I fear you are damned both by father and
mother; thus when I shun Scylla your father, I fall into
15 Charybdis your mother. Well, you are gone both ways.
Jessica
I shall be saved by my husband; he hath made me a
Christian.
Lancelot
Truly, the more to blame he; we were Christians enow
before, e'en as many as could well live one by another.
20 This making of Christians will raise the price of hogs; if
we grow all to be pork eaters, we shall not shortly have a
rasher on the coals for money.

Enter Lorenzo

Jessica
I'll tell my husband, Lancelot, what you say: here he
comes.
Lorenzo
25 I shall grow jealous of you shortly, Lancelot, if you thus
get my wife into corners.
Jessica
Nay, you need not fear us, Lorenzo: Lancelot and I are
out. He tells me flatly there's no mercy for me in heaven,
because I am a Jew's daughter; and he says you are no
30 good member of the commonwealth, for in converting
Jews to Christians you raise the price of pork.
Lorenzo
I shall answer that better to the commonwealth than
you can the getting up of the Negro's belly: the Moor is
with child by you, Lancelot.

Lancelot

35 It is much that the Moor should be more than reason; but if she be less than an honest woman, she is indeed more than I took her for.

Lorenzo

How every fool can play upon the word! I think the best grace of wit will shortly turn into silence, and discourse

40 grow commendable in none only but parrots. Go in, sirrah, bid them prepare for dinner.

Lancelot

That is done, sir; they have all stomachs.

Lorenzo

Goodly Lord, what a witsnapper are you! Then bid them prepare dinner.

Lancelot

45 That is done too, sir; only 'cover' is the word.

Lorenzo

Will you cover then, sir?

Lancelot

Not so, sir, neither; I know my duty.

Lorenzo

Yet more quarrelling with occasion! Wilt thou show the whole wealth of thy wit in an instant? I pray thee

50 understand a plain man in his plain meaning: go to thy fellows, bid them cover the table, serve in the meat, and we will come in to dinner.

Lancelot

For the table, sir, it shall be served in; for the meat, sir, it shall be covered; for your coming in to dinner, sir, why,

55 let it be as humours and conceits shall govern.   [*Exit*

Lorenzo

O dear discretion, how his words are suited!
The fool hath planted in his memory
An army of good words; and I do know
A many fools that stand in better place,

60 Garnish'd like him, that for a tricksy word
Defy the matter. How cheer'st thou, Jessica?
And now, good sweet, say thy opinion:
How dost thou like the Lord Bassanio's wife?

---

35 *more than reason*: bigger than she ought to be; Lancelot cannot resist a pun.
36–7 *if . . . for*: if she's not an honest (= chaste) woman, she's certainly more than I thought she was.
38–40 *the best . . . parrots*: silence will soon be the finest display of intelligence, and only parrots will be praised for conversation.

42 *have all stomachs*: are all hungry.

43 *witsnapper*: punster, comedian.

45 *'cover' . . . word*: you should say 'cover' (meaning a) prepare the table; b) put on your hat).

47 *duty*: place, respect; servants stood bare-headed in the presence of superiors.
48 *quarrelling with occasion*: taking every opportunity for quibbles.

55 *as . . . govern*: as your whims and fancies take you.
56 *discretion*: sagacity, judgement.
suited: matched.
59 *A many fools*: a lot of professional jesters.
stand . . . place: have higher positions.
60 *Garnish'd*: trimmed up; Lorenzo refers to the extra braid on Lancelot's livery (see *2, 2, 144*) which makes him look like a jester.
tricksy: clever, playful.
61 *Defy the matter*: contradict the sense.
How . . . thou: how are you getting on.

64 *Past all expressing*: beyond words.
meet: proper, right.
65 *upright*: virtuous.

73 *Pawn'd*: gambled.
74 *fellow*: equal, match.

77 *anon*: shortly.

78 *stomach*: a) appetite; b) inclination.

79 *table talk*: mealtime conversation.
80 *howsome'er*: however.

81 *set you forth*: put you in your place.

Jessica
Past all expressing. It is very meet
65 The Lord Bassanio live an upright life,
For having such a blessing in his lady
He finds the joys of heaven here on earth,
And if on earth he do not merit it,
In reason he should never come to heaven.
70 Why, if two gods should play some heavenly match,
And on the wager lay two earthly women,
And Portia one, there must be something else
Pawn'd with the other, for the poor rude world
Hath not her fellow.

Lorenzo
                    Even such a husband
75 Hast thou of me, as she is for a wife.

Jessica
Nay, but ask my opinion too of that.

Lorenzo
I will anon; first let us go to dinner.

Jessica
Nay, let me praise you while I have a stomach.

Lorenzo
No, pray thee, let it serve for table talk;
80 Then howsome'er thou speak'st, 'mong other things
I shall digest it.

Jessica
                    Well, I'll set you forth.   [*Exeunt*

ACT 4

Act 4 Scene 1
Antonio is prepared to die when Shylock
refuses to show mercy, but Portia, disguised
as a young lawyer, tricks Shylock out of his
bond. Then she asks Bassanio for his ring
as a reward.

SCENE 1

Venice: the courtroom. Enter the Duke, *the*
Magnificoes, Antonio, Bassanio, Salerio, *and*
Gratiano *with others.*

Duke
What, is Antonio here?
    Antonio
Ready, so please your grace.
    Duke
I am sorry for thee. Thou art come to answer
A stony adversary, an inhuman wretch,
5 Uncapable of pity, void and empty
From any dram of mercy.
    Antonio
                                        I have heard
Your grace hath tane great pains to qualify
His rigorous course; but since he stands obdurate
And that no lawful means can carry me
10 Out of his envy's reach, I do oppose
My patience to his fury, and am arm'd
To suffer with a quietness of spirit
The very tyranny and rage of his.
    Duke
Go one and call the Jew into the court.
    Salerio
15 He is ready at the door; he comes, my lord.

Enter Shylock

Duke
Make room and let him stand before our face.
Shylock, the world thinks, and I think so too,
That thou but leadest this fashion of thy malice
To the last hour of act, and then 'tis thought

2 *Ready*: present.

3 *answer*: defend yourself against.

5 *void*: barren.
6 *From*: of.
  dram: a tiny measure.

7 *qualify*: moderate.
8 *obdurate*: obdùrate; firm, resolute.

10 *envy*: malice.

13 *The . . . his*: all the cruel power and
  anger of his spirit.

18–19 *thou . . . act*: you intend to carry
  on with this show of cruelty until the
  very last moment.

20 *remorse*: pity.
 more strange: even more unusual.
21 *strange apparent*: apparently abnormal.
22 *exacts*: demand.

24 *loose the forfeiture*: surrender the forfeit (i.e. the pound of flesh).

26 *Forgive . . . principal*: forgo a certain amount of the sum he borrowed.

29 *Enow*: enough.
 royal merchant: even such a substantial merchant prince.
30 *commiseration of*: sympathy for.
31 *brassy bosoms*: hearts as hard as brass.
32 *stubborn*: unfeeling.
32–3 *train'd . . . courtesy*: taught to behave with gentleness.
35 *possess'd*: informed.
36 *Sabaoth*: In Hebrew this word means 'armies'; many editions read 'Sabbath' (= Saturday, the holiest day of the Jewish week).
37 *due and forfeit*: forfeit which is due.
38 *light*: alight, descend.
39 *charter . . . freedom*: city's independence granted by charter.
41 *carrion*: rotten.
43 *humour*: whimsy, fancy.
 is it answer'd: will that do for an answer.
46 *ban'd*: poisoned.
47 *gaping pig*: roasted pig's head (with an apple in its mouth).
49 *sings i'the nose*: drones.
50–1 *affection . . . passion*: instinctive (physical) reaction often overcomes emotion (see *3, 1, 53*).
54–6 *he*: this man . . . that man . . . another man.
56 *woollen*: The leather bag of the bagpipes was covered with sheepskin.
 of force: involuntarily.

57 *shame*: embarrassment.
58 *to offend*: give offence to others.

20 Thou'lt show thy mercy and remorse more strange
Than is thy strange apparent cruelty.
And where thou now exacts the penalty,
Which is a pound of this poor merchant's flesh,
Thou wilt not only loose the forfeiture
25 But, touch'd with human gentleness and love,
Forgive a moiety of the principal,
Glancing an eye of pity on his losses
That have of late so huddl'd on his back,
Enow to press a royal merchant down
30 And pluck commiseration of his state
From brassy bosoms and rough hearts of flint,
From stubborn Turks, and Tartars never train'd
To offices of tender courtesy.
We all expect a gentle answer, Jew.
  Shylock
35 I have possess'd your grace of what I purpose,
And by our holy Sabaoth have I sworn
To have the due and forfeit of my bond.
If you deny it, let the danger light
Upon your charter and your city's freedom!
40 You'll ask me why I rather choose to have
A weight of carrion flesh than to receive
Three thousand ducats. I'll not answer that—
But say it is my humour: is it answer'd?
What if my house be troubled with a rat,
45 And I be pleas'd to give ten thousand ducats
To have it ban'd? What, are you answer'd yet?
Some men there are love not a gaping pig;
Some that are mad if they behold a cat;
And others when the bagpipe sings i'the nose
50 Cannot contain their urine: for affection
Masters oft passion, sways it to the mood
Of what it likes or loathes. Now for your answer:
As there is no firm reason to be render'd
Why he cannot abide a gaping pig,
55 Why he a harmless necessary cat,
Why he a woollen bagpipe, but of force
Must yield to such inevitable shame
As to offend, himself being offended:
So can I give no reason, nor I will not,

60 *lodg'd*: deep-rooted. *certain*: steadfast.	60 More than a lodg'd hate and a certain loathing
	I bear Antonio, that I follow thus
62 *losing*: unprofitable.	A losing suit against him. Are you answer'd?
	Bassanio
	This is no answer, thou unfeeling man,
64 *current*: outpouring.	To excuse the current of thy cruelty.
	Shylock
	65 I am not bound to please thee with my answers.
	Bassanio
	Do all men kill the things they do not love?
	Shylock
	Hates any man the thing he would not kill?
	Bassanio
68 *offence*: displeasure.	Every offence is not a hate at first.
	Shylock
	What, wouldst thou have a serpent sting thee twice?
	Antonio
70 *think . . . Jew*: remember that you are arguing with the Jew.	70 I pray you think you question with the Jew.
	You may as well go stand upon the beach
72 *main flood*: ocean tide. *bate*: reduce.	And bid the main flood bate his usual height;
73 *use question with*: ask.	You may as well use question with the wolf
	Why he hath made the ewe bleat for the lamb;
	75 You may as well forbid the mountain pines
	To wag their high tops and to make no noise
77 *fretten*: blown.	When they are fretten with the gusts of heaven;
	You may as well do anything most hard
	As seek to soften that—than which what's harder?—
	80 His Jewish heart. Therefore I do beseech you
	Make no moe offers, use no farther means,
82 *with . . . conveniency*: as quickly and simply as possible.	But with all brief and plain conveniency
	Let me have judgement, and the Jew his will.
	Bassanio
	For thy three thousand ducats here is six.
	Shylock
	85 If every ducat in six thousand ducats
	Were in six parts, and every part a ducat,
87 *draw*: take.	I would not draw them; I would have my bond.
	Duke
	How shalt thou hope for mercy, rendering none?
	Shylock
	What judgement shall I dread, doing no wrong?

90   You have among you many a purchas'd slave,
Which, like your asses and your dogs and mules,
You use in abject and in slavish parts
Because you bought them. Shall I say to you,
'Let them be free! Marry them to your heirs!
95   Why sweat they under burdens? Let their beds
Be made as soft as yours, and let their palates
Be season'd with such viands'? You will answer,
'The slaves are ours.' So do I answer you.
The pound of flesh which I demand of him
100   Is dearly bought; 'tis mine, and I will have it.
If you deny me, fie upon your law:
There is no force in the decrees of Venice.
I stand for judgement. Answer: shall I have it?

Duke
Upon my power I may dismiss this court,
105   Unless Bellario, a learned doctor
Whom I have sent for to determine this,
Come here today.

Salerio
                    My lord, here stays without
A messenger with letters from the doctor,
New come from Padua.

Duke
110   Bring us the letters. Call the messenger.

Bassanio
Good cheer, Antonio! What, man, courage yet!
The Jew shall have my flesh, blood, bones and all,
Ere thou shalt lose for me one drop of blood.

Antonio
I am a tainted wether of the flock,
115   Meetest for death; the weakest kind of fruit
Drops earliest to the ground, and so let me.
You cannot better be employ'd, Bassanio,
Than to live still and write mine epitaph.

Enter Nerissa *disguised as a lawyer's clerk*

Duke
Came you from Padua, from Bellario?

Nerissa

120 From both, my lord: [*Presenting letter*] Bellario greets
       your grace.

Bassanio

Why dost thou whet thy knife so earnestly?

Shylock

To cut the forfeiture from that bankrupt there.

Gratiano

Not on thy sole, but on thy soul, harsh Jew,
Thou mak'st thy knife keen. But no metal can,
125 No, not the hangman's axe, bear half the keenness
Of thy sharp envy. Can no prayers pierce thee?

Shylock

No, none that thou hast wit enough to make.

Gratiano

O be thou damn'd, inexecrable dog,
And for thy life let justice be accus'd!
130 Thou almost mak'st me waver in my faith,
To hold opinion with Pythagoras
That souls of animals infuse themselves
Into the trunks of men. Thy currish spirit
Govern'd a wolf, who—hang'd for human slaughter—
135 Even from the gallows did his fell soul fleet,
And whilst thou layest in thy unhallow'd dam
Infus'd itself in thee; for thy desires
Are wolfish, bloody, starv'd, and ravenous.

Shylock

Till thou canst rail the seal from off my bond
140 Thou but offend'st thy lungs to speak so loud.
Repair thy wit, good youth, or it will fall
To cureless ruin. I stand here for law.

Duke

This letter from Bellario doth commend
A young and learned doctor to our court:
145 Where is he?

Nerissa

                        He attendeth here hard by
To know your answer whether you'll admit him.

---

121 *whet*: sharpen.

123 *thy sole*: the sole of your shoe.

125 *hangman*: executioner.

127 *wit*: sense, intelligence.

128 *inexecrable*: unspeakably damned.

129 *for . . . accus'd*: only a failure of justice allows you to live.
131 *hold opinion*: agree.
Pythagoras: a Greek philosopher who believed in the transmigration of souls—explained here by Gratiano.
132 *infuse*: pour.
133 *currish*: like a cur—a mongrel dog.
134 *hang'd . . . slaughter*: executed as a murderer.
135 *Even . . . fleet*: let his cruel soul pass straight from the gallows.
136 *unhallow'd dam*: unholy (non-Christian) mother.

139 *rail*: shout.
140 *but offend'st*: are only hurting.

142 *cureless*: incurable.

145 *hard*: near.

Duke

With all my heart. Some three of four of you

Go give him courteous conduct to this place.

[*Exeunt* officials

Meantime the court shall hear Bellario's letter.

150 [*Reads*] 'Your grace shall understand, that at the receipt

of your letter I am very sick; but in the instant that your

messenger came, in loving visitation was with me a

young doctor of Rome: his name is Balthazar. I

acquainted him with the cause in controversy between

155 the Jew and Antonio the merchant. We turned o'er

many books together; he is furnished with my opinion

which, bettered with his own learning, the greatness

whereof I cannot enough commend, comes with him at

my importunity, to fill up your grace's request in my

160 stead. I beseech you let his lack of years be no

impediment to let him lack a reverend estimation, for I

never knew so young a body with so old a head. I leave

him to your gracious acceptance, whose trial shall better

publish his commendation.'

Enter Portia *disguised as* Doctor Balthazar, *followed
by* officials

165 You hear the learn'd Bellario what he writes,

And here I take it is the doctor come.

Give me your hand. Come you from old Bellario?

Portia

I did, my lord.

Duke

You are welcome; take your place.

Are you acquainted with the difference

170 That holds this present question in the court?

Portia

I am informed throughly of the cause.

Which is the merchant here and which the Jew?

Duke

Antonio and old Shylock, both stand forth.

Portia

Is your name Shylock?

---

148 *give . . . conduct*: escort him courteously.

152 *in loving visitation*: on a friendly visit.

154 *cause*: matter.
controversy: dispute.
155 *turned o'er*: looked through.
156 *is furnished*: has been given.
157 *bettered*: improved.

159 *importunity*: earnest request.

160–1 *let . . . estimation*: do not think poorly of him because he is young.

163–4 *whose . . . commendation*: giving him a trial will show you how much better he is than my praise.

169–70 *the difference . . . court*: the dispute that is at present on trial in this court.

171 *informed*: informèd.
throughly: thoroughly.

Shylock

Shylock is my name.

Portia

175 Of a strange nature is the suit you follow,

Yet in such rule that the Venetian law

Cannot impugn you as you do proceed.

—You stand within his danger, do you not?

Antonio

Ay, so he says.

Portia

Do you confess the bond?

Antonio

180 I do.

Portia

Then must the Jew be merciful.

Shylock

On what compulsion must I? Tell me that.

Portia

The quality of mercy is not strain'd,

It droppeth as the gentle rain from heaven

Upon the place beneath. It is twice blest:

185 It blesseth him that gives, and him that takes.

'Tis mightiest in the mightiest, it becomes

The thronèd monarch better than his crown.

His sceptre shows the force of temporal power,

The attribute to awe and majesty,

190 Wherein doth sit the dread and fear of kings;

But mercy is above this sceptred sway.

It is enthronèd in the hearts of kings,

It is an attribute to God himself,

And early power doth then show likest God's

195 When mercy seasons justice. Therefore, Jew,

Though justice be thy plea, consider this:

That in the course of justice, none of us

Should see salvation. We do pray for mercy,

And that same prayer doth teach us all to render

200 The deeds of mercy. I have spoke thus much

To mitigate the justice of thy plea,

Which if thou follow, this strict court of Venice

Must needs give sentence 'gainst the merchant there.

176 *in such rule*: so correctly.

177 *impugn*: oppose.

178 *within his danger*: at his mercy.

180 *must*: is morally obliged to.

181 *must I*: am I forced to.

182 *is not strain'd*: cannot be constrained (= forced).

186 *mightiest . . . mightiest*: the most powerful weapon possessed by the most powerful person.
becomes: suits, is appropriate for.

187 *throned*: thronèd.

188 *temporal*: earthly.

189 *attribute*: proper possession.

190 *Wherein . . . kings*: in which (symbolically) resides the power of kings to command dread and fear.

191 *this sceptred sway*: the world ruled by kings.

192 *enthroned*: enthronèd.

193 *attribute to*: quality belonging to.

195 *seasons*: moderates.

195–200 *Therefore . . . mercy*: Portia reminds Christians of the petition of the Lord's Prayer ('Forgive us our trespasses as we forgive them that trespass against us'), and Shylock should remember Psalm 143:2 ('Enter not into judgement with thy servants: for in thy sight shall no man living be justified').

201 *mitigate . . . plea*: moderate your plea for strict justice.

203 *needs*: of necessity.

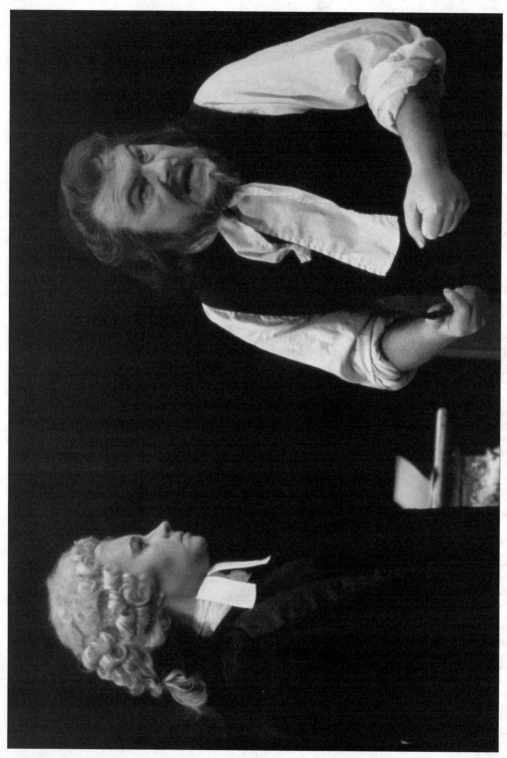

'I crave the law, The penalty and forfeit of my bond.' (*4*, 1, 204–5). Prunella Scales as Portia and Timothy West as Shylock, Old Vic Theatre, 1981.

Shylock
My deeds upon my head! I crave the law,
205 The penalty and forfeit of my bond.
    Portia
Is he not able to discharge the money?
    Bassanio
Yes, here I tender it for him in the court,
Yea, twice the sum; if that will not suffice,
I will be bound to pay it ten times o'er
210 On forfeit of my hands, my head, my heart.
If this will not suffice, it must appear
That malice bears down truth. And I beseech you
Wrest once the law to your authority;
To do a great right, do a little wrong,
215 And curb this cruel devil of his will.
    Portia
It must not be; there is no power in Venice
Can alter a decree established.
'Twill be recorded for a precedent,
And many an error by the same example
220 Will rush into the state: it cannot be.
    Shylock
A Daniel come to judgement; yea a Daniel!
O wise young judge, how I do honour thee!
    Portia
I pray you let me look upon the bond.
    Shylock
Here 'tis, most reverend doctor, here it is.
    Portia
225 Shylock, there's thrice thy money offer'd thee.
    Shylock
An oath, an oath. I have an oath in heaven!
Shall I lay perjury upon my soul?
No, not for Venice.
    Portia
                                Why, this bond is forfeit,
And lawfully by this the Jew may claim
230 A pound of flesh, to be by him cut off
Nearest the merchant's heart. Be merciful:
Take thrice thy money; bid me tear the bond.

204 *My . . . head*: I will be responsible for
    what I am doing.
    crave: beg.

206 *discharge*: repay.

207 *tender*: offer.

212 *bears down*: overcomes.

213 *Wrest*: twist.
    once: on this one occasion.
    to: with.
215 *curb*: restrain.

217 *established*: establishèd.

221 *Daniel*: The story of Susannah and the
    Elders in the Apocrypha tells how a
    young man, sent to give judgement
    when Susannah was accused of
    unchastity, turned the evidence of the
    old men against themselves.

225 *thrice*: Portia seems to be raising the
    offer of line 208.

233 *tenour*: actual wording.

235 *exposition*: setting-out, explanation.

237 *pillar*: support.

240 *stay*: take my stand.

241 *Most heartily*: with all my heart.

246 *Hath . . . to*: fully authorizes.

249 *elder*: more mature.

253 *balance*: scales.

255 *on your charge*: at your expense.
257 *nominated*: specified.

Shylock
When it is paid, according to the tenour.
It doth appear you are a worthy judge,
235 You know the law, your exposition
Hath been most sound. I charge you by the law,
Whereof you are a well-deserving pillar,
Proceed to judgement. By my soul I swear
There is no power in the tongue of man
240 To alter me. I stay here on my bond.
    Antonio
Most heartily I do beseech the court
To give the judgement.
        Portia
                                Why then, thus it is:
You must prepare your bosom for his knife.
        Shylock
O noble judge, O excellent young man!
        Portia
245 For the intent and purpose of the law
Hath full relation to the penalty
Which here appeareth due upon the bond.
        Shylock
'Tis very true. O wise and upright judge,
How much more elder art thou than thy looks!
        Portia
250 Therefore lay bare your bosom
        Shylock
                                Ay, his breast.
So says the bond, doth it not, noble judge?
'Nearest his heart': those are the very words.
        Portia
It is so. Are there balance here to weigh
The flesh?
        Shylock
                I have them ready.
        Portia
255 Have by some surgeon, Shylock, on your charge,
To stop his wounds, lest he do bleed to death.
        Shylock
Is it so nominated in the bond?

Portia
It is not so express'd, but what of that?
'Twere good you do so much for charity.
       Shylock
260 I cannot find it; 'tis not in the bond.
       Portia
You, merchant: have you anything to say?
       Antonio
But little; I am arm'd and well prepar'd.
Give me your hand, Bassanio. Fare you well.
Grieve not that I am fall'n to this for you.
265 For herein Fortune shows herself more kind
Than is her custom: it is still her use
To let the wretched man outlive his wealth,
To view with hollow eye and wrinkled brow
An age of poverty; from which ling'ring penance
270 Of such misery doth she cut me off.
Commend me to your honourable wife.
Tell her the process of Antonio's end,
Say how I lov'd you, speak me fair in death,
And when the tale is told, bid her be judge
275 Whether Bassanio had not once a love.
Repent but you that you shall lose your friend
And he repents not that he pays your debt.
For if the Jew do cut but deep enough
I'll pay it instantly with all my heart.
       Bassanio
280 Antonio, I am married to a wife
Which is as dear to me as life itself;
But life itself, my wife, and all the world,
Are not with me esteem'd above thy life.
I would lose all, ay, sacrifice them all
285 Here to this devil, to deliver you.
       Portia
Your wife would give you little thanks for that
If she were by to hear you make the offer.
       Gratiano
I have a wife who I protest I love;
I would she were in heaven, so she could
290 Entreat some power to change this currish Jew.

262 *arm'd*: i.e. spiritually.

266 *still her use*: usually her custom.

269 *age*: old age.

272 *process*: a) manner; b) legal proceeding.
273 *speak . . . death*: speak kindly of me when I am dead.

276 *Repent but you*: you must only regret.

281 *Which*: who.

285 *deliver*: save.

'Most learned judge! A sentence: come, prepare.' (*4*, 1, 302). Geraldine James as Portia, Leigh Lawson as Antonio, and Dustin Hoffman as Shylock, Phoenix Theatre, 1989.

Nerissa
'Tis well you offer it behind her back;
The wish would make else an unquiet house.
    Shylock
These be the Christian husbands! I have a daughter:
Would any of the stock of Barabbas
295 Had been her husband, rather than a Christian!
We trifle time; I pray thee pursue sentence.
    Portia
A pound of that same merchant's flesh is thine,
The court awards it, and the law doth give it.
    Shylock
Most rightful judge!
    Portia
300 And you must cut this flesh from off his breast;
The law allows it, and the court awards it.
    Shylock
Most learned judge! A sentence: come, prepare.
    Portia
Tarry a little, there is something else.
This bond doth give thee here no jot of blood.
305 The words expressly are 'a pound of flesh'.
Take then thy bond, take thou thy pound of flesh,
But in the cutting it, if thou dost shed
One drop of Christian blood, thy lands and goods
Are by the laws of Venice confiscate
310 Unto the state of Venice.
    Gratiano
                    O upright judge!
Mark, Jew—O learned judge!
    Shylock
Is that the law?
    Portia
               Thyself shall see the Act.
For as thou urgest justice, be assur'd
Thou shalt have justice more than thou desirest.
    Gratiano
315 O learned judge! Mark, Jew: a learned judge.
    Shylock
I take this offer then. Pay the bond thrice
And let the Christian go.

---

294 *stock*: breed.
   Barabbas: the thief who was released when Christ was crucified (St John 18:40).
296 *trifle time*: waste time in trivialities.
   pursue: go on with.

303 *Tarry*: wait.
304 *jot*: drop.

312 *Act*: the legal act confirming the law.
313 *urgest*: demand.

Bassanio
                                    Here is the money.
Portia
Soft.
The Jew shall have all justice; soft, no haste;
320 He shall have nothing but the penalty.
Gratiano
O Jew, an upright judge, a learned judge!
Portia
Therefore prepare thee to cut off the flesh.
Shed thou no blood, nor cut thou less nor more
But just a pound of flesh. If thou tak'st more
325 Or less than a just pound, be it but so much
As makes it light or heavy in the substance
Or the division of the twentieth part
Of one poor scruple—nay, if the scale do turn
But in the estimation of a hair,
330 Thou diest, and all thy goods are confiscate.
Gratiano
A second Daniel; a Daniel, Jew!
Now, infidel, I have you on the hip.
Portia
Why doth the Jew pause? Take thy forfeiture.
Shylock
Give me my principal, and let me go.
Bassanio
335 I have it ready for thee; here it is.
Portia
He hath refus'd it in the open court.
He shall have merely justice and his bond.
Gratiano
A Daniel, still say I, a second Daniel!
I thank thee, Jew, for teaching me that word.
Shylock
340 Shall I not have barely my principal?
Portia
Thou shalt have nothing but the forfeiture,
To be so taken at thy peril, Jew.
Shylock
Why then, the devil give him good of it!
I'll stay no longer question.

321 *upright*: honest.

326 *substance*: weight.

328 *scruple*: a weight unit (used by the old apothecaries) of 20 grains.
329 *estimation*: weight.

332 *on the hip*: at a disadvantage; see *1*, 3, 41.

334 *principal*: the original sum borrowed.

344 *question*: to argue.

Portia

Tarry, Jew:

345 The law hath yet another hold on you.

It is enacted in the laws of Venice,

If it be prov'd against an alien

That by direct or indirect attempts

He seek the life of any citizen,

350 The party 'gainst the which he doth contrive

Shall seize one half his goods, the other half

Comes to the privy coffer of the state,

And the offender's life lies in the mercy

Of the duke only, 'gainst all other voice.

355 In which predicament I say thou stand'st;

For it appears by manifest proceeding

That indirectly, and directly too,

Thou hast contriv'd against the very life

Of the defendant, and thou hast incurr'd

360 The danger formerly by me rehears'd.

Down, therefore, and beg mercy of the duke.

Gratiano

Beg that thou mayst have leave to hang thyself—

And yet, thy wealth being forfeit to the state,

Thou hast not left the value of a cord;

365 Therefore thou must be hang'd at the state's charge.

Duke

That thou shalt see the difference of our spirit,

I pardon thee thy life before thou ask it.

For half thy wealth, it is Antonio's;

The other half comes to the general state,

370 Which humbleness may drive unto a fine.

Portia

Ay, for the state, not for Antonio.

Shylock

Nay, take my life and all, pardon not that:

You take my house when you do take the prop

That doth sustain my house; you take my life

375 When you do take the means whereby I live.

Portia

What mercy can you render him, Antonio?

Gratiano

A halter gratis—nothing else, for God's sake.

346 *enacted*: decreed.

350 *party*: person (Portia uses the correct legal term, still used today). *contrive*: plot.
351 *seize*: take possession of.
352 *privy coffer*: treasury.

354 *'gainst . . . voice*: without appeal.

356 *manifest proceeding*: quite clearly from what has happened.

360 *rehears'd*: declared.

369 *general state*: general use of the state.
370 *Which . . . fine*: which your good behaviour may reduce to a fine.

371 *not for Antonio*: not Antonio's share of the money.

377 *halter*: rope to hang himself with. *gratis*: free of interest.

Antonio

So please my lord the duke and all the court
To quit the fine for one half of his goods,
380 I am content, so he will let me have
The other half in use, to render it
Upon his death unto the gentleman
That lately stole his daughter.
Two things provided more: that for this favour
385 He presently become a Christian;
The other, that he do record a gift,
Here in the court, of all he dies possess'd
Unto his son Lorenzo and his daughter.

Duke

He shall do this, or else I do recant
390 The pardon that I late pronounced here.

Portia

Art thou contented, Jew? What dost thou say?

Shylock

I am content.

Portia

                              Clerk, draw a deed of gift.

Shylock

I pray you give me leave to go from hence;
I am not well. Send the deed after me
395 And I will sign it.

Duke

                              Get thee gone, but do it.

Gratiano

In christening shalt thou have two godfathers:
Had I been judge, thou shouldst have had ten more
To bring thee to the gallows, not to the font.

[*Exit* Shylock

Duke

Sir, I entreat you home with me to dinner.

Portia

400 I humbly do desire your grace of pardon.
I must away this night toward Padua,
And it is meet I presently set forth.

---

378 *So please*: if it pleases.
379 *quit*: be satisfied with. *for*: instead of.
380 *so*: provided that.
381 *in use*: on trust—to use as Antonio now describes.
385 *presently*: immediately.
386 *record a gift*: sign a legal deed of gift.
387 *all he dies possess'd*: all that he owns when he dies.
389 *recant*: withdraw.
390 *pronounced*: pronouncèd.
396 *godfathers*: sponsors who would guarantee Christian upbringing (for an infant).
397 *ten more*: i.e. enough to constitute a jury.
402 *meet*: necessary.

403 *your leisure serves you not*: you do not
  have time to spare.
404 *gratify*: show your gratitude to.
405 *bound*: indebted.

407–8 *acquitted Of*: set free from.

408 *in lieu whereof*: in payment for this.

410 *freely*: most willingly.
  cope: reward.
  pains: trouble.
411 *over and above*: in addition.

416 *mercenary*: interested in money.
417 *know*: recognize.

419 *of force*: it is necessary.
  attempt you further: try harder to
  persuade you.
420 *some remembrance*: something to
  remind you.
  tribute: token of respect.

423 *You press me far*: you are very
  insistent.
424 *for your sake*: to acknowledge your
  politeness.
425 *for your love*: to acknowledge your
  love.

431 *have . . . it*: really want it.

Duke
I am sorry that your leisure serves you not.
Antonio, gratify this gentleman,
405 For in my mind you are much bound to him.

  [*Exit* Duke *and his train*

Bassanio
Most worthy gentleman, I and my friend
Have by your wisdom been this day acquitted
Of grievous penalties, in lieu whereof
Three thousand ducats due unto the Jew
410 We freely cope your courteous pains withal.

Antonio
And stand indebted over and above
In love and service to you evermore.

Portia
He is well paid that is well satisfied;
And I delivering you am satisfied
415 And therein do account myself well paid;
My mind was never yet more mercenary.
I pray you know me when we meet again.
I wish you well, and so I take my leave.

Bassanio
Dear sir, of force I must attempt you further.
420 Take some remembrance of us as a tribute,
Not as a fee. Grant me two things, I pray you:
Not to deny me, and to pardon me.

Portia
You press me far, and therefore I will yield.
Give me your gloves, I'll wear them for your sake;
425 And for your love I'll take this ring from you.
Do not draw back your hand; I'll take no more,
And you in love shall not deny me this.

Bassanio
This ring, good sir? Alas, it is a trifle;
I will not shame myself to give you this.

Portia
430 I will have nothing else but only this;
And now methinks I have a mind to it.

Bassanio
There's more depends on this than on the value.

'In christening shalt thou have two godfathers' (*4*, 1, 396). Nicholas Farrell as Bassanio, Antony Sher as Shylock, and Geoffrey Freshwater as Gratiano, Royal Shakespeare Company, 1988.

434 *proclamation*: public announcement.

435 *this*: this one.

436 *liberal in offers*: only generous in
making offers (without fulfilling
them).

442 *scuse*: excuse.

449 *'gainst*: in balance with.
commandement: commandèment: a
four-syllable word is necessary for the
rhythm.

The dearest ring in Venice will I give you,
And find it out by proclamation.
435 Only for this I pray you pardon me.
    Portia
I see, sir, you are liberal in offers.
You taught me first to beg, and now methinks
You teach me how a beggar should be answer'd.
    Bassanio
Good sir, this ring was given me by my wife,
440 And when she put it on, she made me vow
That I should neither sell, nor give, nor lose it.
    Portia
That scuse serves many men to save their gifts;
And if your wife be not a mad woman,
And know how well I have deserv'd this ring,
445 She would not hold out enemy for ever
For giving it to me. Well, peace be with you.
                 [*Exeunt* Portia *and* Nerissa
    Antonio
My lord Bassanio, let him have the ring.
Let his deservings and my love withal
Be valu'd 'gainst your wife's commandement.
    Bassanio
450 Go, Gratiano, run and overtake him;
Give him the ring, and bring him if thou canst
Unto Antonio's house. Away, make haste.
                 [*Exit* Gratiano
Come, you and I will thither presently,
And in the morning early will we both
455 Fly toward Belmont. Come, Antonio.   [*Exeunt*

Act 4 Scene 2
Portia gets Bassanio's ring—and Nerissa
plans to get her own from Gratiano.

1 *Enquire . . . out*: find out where the
Jew's house is.
this deed: the document in which he
promises to make Lorenzo his heir.

5 *well o'ertane*: I'm glad I've caught up
with you.
6 *upon more advice*: having thought
more about the matter.

15 *Thou . . . warrant*: I'm sure you'll
succeed.
old: extraordinary.

18 *tarry*: wait.

SCENE 2

Venice: a street. Enter Portia *and* Nerissa

Portia
Enquire the Jew's house out, give him this deed,
And let him sign it. We'll away tonight
And be a day before our husbands home.
This deed will be well welcome to Lorenzo.

Enter Gratiano

Gratiano
5 Fair sir, you are well o'ertane.
My lord Bassanio upon more advice
Hath sent you here this ring, and doth entreat
Your company at dinner.
Portia
                    That cannot be.
His ring I do accept most thankfully,
10 And so I pray you tell him. Furthermore,
I pray you show my youth old Shylock's house.
    Gratiano
That will I do.
    Nerissa
[*To* Portia]   Sir, I would speak with you.
[*Aside*] I'll see if I can get my husband's ring
Which I did make him swear to keep for ever.
    Portia
15 Thou mayst, I warrant. We shall have old swearing
That they did give the rings away to men;
But we'll outface them, and outswear them too.
—Away, make haste, thou know'st where I will tarry.
    Nerissa
Come, good sir, will you show me to this house?
                                        [*Exeunt*

Act 5 Scene 1
Lorenzo teases Jessica as they wait in the moonlight. Portia and Nerissa return from Venice, followed by Bassanio and Gratiano—who are embarrassed when their wives demand to see the rings. All is explained, and Portia has good news for Antonio.

4–6 *Troilus . . . night*: In the Trojan War Troilus was separated from Cressida when she was taken to the Greek camp; their love is the subject of Chaucer's *Troylus and Criseyde* and Shakespeare's *Troilus and Cressida*.

7, 10, 13 *Thisbe . . . Dido . . . Medea*: Their stories are told in Chaucer's *Legend of Good Women*.

7 *Thisbe*: When Thisbe, frightened by a lion, failed to keep her assignation, her grieving lover Pyramus killed himself; a (comic) version of the episode is presented in *A Midsummer's Night's Dream*.
o'ertrip: trip across.

8 *ere himself*: before she saw him.

10 *Dido*: The Queen of Carthage, deserted by her lover Aeneas, was the protagonist of a tragedy by Shakespeare's contemporary, Christopher Marlowe.
willow: The traditional emblem of forsaken love.

11 *waft*: beckoned.

13–14 *Medea . . . Aeson*: When she had helped Jason on his voyage to win the Golden Fleece (see *1, 1, 170* note), the enchantress Medea gave Aeson, his father, a rejuvenating herbal potion.

15 *steal*: a) creep away; b) rob.

16 *unthrift*: a) careless, prodigal; b) penniless.

19 *Stealing her soul*: a) gaining possession of her love; b) converting her away from her Jewish faith.

Scene 1

Belmont: the garden. Enter Lorenzo *and* Jessica

Lorenzo
The moon shines bright. In such a night as this,
When the sweet wind did gently kiss the trees,
And they did make no noise, in such a night
Troilus methinks mounted the Troyan walls
5 And sigh'd his soul toward the Grecian tents,
Where Cressid lay that night.
Jessica
                                            In such a night
Did Thisbe fearfully o'ertrip the dew,
And saw the lion's shadow ere himself,
And ran dismay'd away.
Lorenzo
                                            In such a night
10 Stood Dido with a willow in her hand
Upon the wild sea banks, and waft her love
To come again to Carthage.
Jessica
                                            In such a night
Medea gather'd the enchanted herbs
That did renew old Aeson.
Lorenzo
                                            In such a night
15 Did Jessica steal from the wealthy Jew
And with an unthrift love did run from Venice
As far as Belmont.
Jessica
                                            In such a night
Did young Lorenzo swear he lov'd her well,
Stealing her soul with many vows of faith,
20 And ne'er a true one.

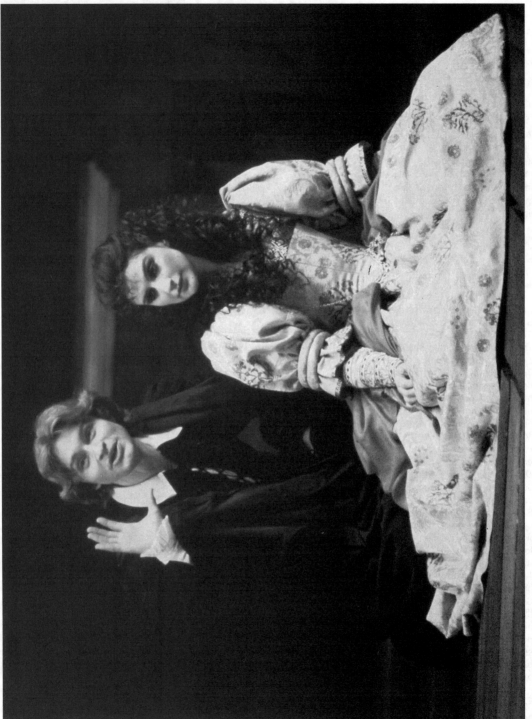

'In such a night Did Jessica steal from the wealthy Jew' (5, 1, 14–15). Paul Spence as Lorenzo and Deborah Goodman as Jessica, Royal Shakespeare Company, 1987.

21 *shrew*: scolding woman.

23 *outnight you*: i.e. beat you at this game.
did nobody come: if there were not somebody coming.

30–2 *She . . . hours*: This apparent change of plan (*3*, 4, 26–32) passes unnoticed in the theatre.
31 *holy crosses*: wayside shrines.

37–8 *ceremoniously . . . welcome*: let us prepare some ceremony of welcome.

39 *Sola . . . sola*: Lancelot pretends that he cannot find Lorenzo.

Lorenzo
                                    In such a night
Did pretty Jessica (like a little shrew)
Slander her love, and he forgave it her.
Jessica
I would outnight you, did nobody come:
But hark, I hear the footing of a man.

Enter Stephano, *a messenger*

Lorenzo
25 Who comes so fast in silence of the night?
Stephano
A friend.
Lorenzo
A friend? What friend? Your name, I pray you, friend?
Stephano
Stephano is my name, and I bring word
My mistress will before the break of day
30 Be here at Belmont. She doth stray about
By holy crosses where she kneels and prays
For happy wedlock hours.
Lorenzo
                                    Who comes with her?
Stephano
None but a holy hermit and her maid.
I pray you, is my master yet return'd?
Lorenzo
35 He is not, nor we have not heard from him.
But go we in, I pray thee, Jessica,
And ceremoniously let us prepare
Some welcome for the mistress of the house.

Enter Lancelot, *the Clown*

Lancelot
Sola, sola! Wo ha, ho! Sola, sola!
Lorenzo
40 Who calls?

Lancelot
Sola! Did you see Master Lorenzo? Master Lorenzo, sola, sola!
Lorenzo
Leave holloaing, man! Here!
Lancelot
Sola! Where, where?
Lorenzo
45 Here!
Lancelot
Tell him there's a post come from my master, with his horn full of good news: my master will be here ere morning, sweet soul.
Lorenzo
Let's in and there expect their coming.
50 And yet no matter: why should we go in?
My friend Stephano, signify I pray you,
Within the house, your mistress is at hand,
And bring your music forth into the air.
        [*Exit* Stephano
How sweet the moonlight sleeps upon this bank!
55 Here will we sit, and let the sounds of music
Creep in our ears; soft stillness and the night
Become the touches of sweet harmony.
Sit, Jessica. Look how the floor of heaven
Is thick inlaid with patens of bright gold.
60 There's not the smallest orb which thou behold'st
But in his motion like an angel sings,
Still choiring to the young-eyed cherubins.
Such harmony is in immortal souls,
But whilst this muddy vesture of decay
65 Doth grossly close it in, we cannot hear it.

Enter Stephano *with musicians*

Come, ho! and wake Diana with a hymn.
With sweetest touches pierce your mistress' ear,
And draw her home with music.

Music plays

---

43 *Leave holloaing*: stop shouting.

46 *post*: courier.
47 *horn . . . news*: i.e. like a cornucopia (= horn of plenty).
48 *sweet soul*: Many editors place these words at the beginning of line 49 (which is two syllables short of a regular pentameter).

51 *signify*: announce.

53 *your music*: the resident musicians.

57 *Become*: suit, befit.

59 *patens*: little metal plates (used in Holy Communion).
60-1 *There's . . . sings*: The Elizabethans believed that heavenly harmony was created by the movement of the planets ('orbs').
62 *Still choiring*: always singing together. *young-eyed cherubins*: Elizabethans imagined these angelic creatures (see Ezekiel 10:12) as beautiful winged children.
63 *Such*: the same.
64 *muddy . . . decay*: clothing of mortality made from the dust of the earth (Genesis 2:7).
65 *grossly*: roughly, crudely.
66 *wake Diana*: call out the moon (which seems in line 109 to have gone behind a cloud).

Jessica
I am never merry when I hear sweet music.
   Lorenzo
70 The reason is your spirits are attentive.
For do but note a wild and wanton herd
Or race of youthful and unhandled colts
Fetching mad bounds, bellowing and neighing loud—
Which is the hot condition of their blood—
75 If they but hear perchance a trumpet sound,
Or any air of music touch their ears,
You shall perceive them make a mutual stand,
Their savage eyes turn'd to a modest gaze
By the sweet power of music. Therefore the poet
80 Did feign that Orpheus drew trees, stones, and floods;
Since naught so stockish, hard, and full of rage,
But music for the time doth change his nature.
The man that hath no music in himself,
Nor is not mov'd with concord of sweet sounds,
85 Is fit for treasons, stratagems, and spoils;
The motions of his spirit are dull as night
And his affections dark as Erebus.
Let no such man be trusted. Mark the music.

Enter Portia *and* Nerissa

   Portia
That light we see is burning in my hall.
90 How far that little candle throws his beams!
So shines a good deed in a naughty world.
   Nerissa
When the moon shone we did not see the candle.
   Portia
So doth the greater glory dim the less:
A substitute shines brightly as a king
95 Until a king be by, and then his state
Empties itself, as doth an inland brook
Into the main of waters. Music, hark!
   Nerissa
It is your music, madam, of the house.

72 *race*: herd, stud.
  unhandled: unbroken, untrained.

74 *hot . . . blood*: nature of their excited spirit.
75 *perchance*: perhaps.

77 *make . . . stand*: all stand still at once.
78 *modest*: gentle.
79–80 *the poet . . . floods*: the Roman poet Ovid told how Orpheus, a Greek musician, charmed even lifeless objects with his music.
81 *naught*: nothing.
  stockish: stubborn.

84 *concord*: harmony.

85 *stratagems*: plots.
  spoils: destruction.
86 *motions*: movements.
87 *Erebus*: the place of darkness in the classical underworld.
88 *Mark*: pay attention to.

91 *naughty*: wicked.

94 *substitute*: deputy.

95 *by*: present.
95–6 *his . . . itself*: his glory vanishes.

97 *main of waters*: sea.

98 *your . . . house*: the resident musicians.

99 *Nothing . . . respect*: i.e. everything is relative to something else.

101 *virtue*: special quality.

103 *attended*: listened to.

104 *nightingale*: A bird that sings only at night, when all other birds are silent.

107 *by . . . are*: are given a better flavour by coming at the proper time.

109 *the moon . . . Endymion*: Diana, goddess of the moon, slept on Mount Latmos with her love, the shepherd-boy Endymion.

115 *speed*: prosper.

119–20 *take . . . note*: make no mention.

121s.d. *tucket*: personal trumpet call.

Portia
Nothing is good, I see, without respect;
100 Methinks it sounds much sweeter than by day.
   Nerissa
Silence bestows that virtue on it, madam.
   Portia
The crow doth sing as sweetly as the lark
When neither is attended; and I think
The nightingale, if she should sing by day
105 When every goose is cackling, would be thought
No better a musician than the wren.
How many things by season season'd are
To their right praise and true perfection.
Peace, ho! The moon sleeps with Endymion
110 And would not be awak'd!

Music ceases

Lorenzo
                              That is the voice
Or I am much deceiv'd, of Portia!
   Portia
He knows me as the blind man knows the cuckoo
By the bad voice.
   Lorenzo
                       Dear lady, welcome home!
   Portia
We have been praying for our husbands' welfare,
115 Which speed we hope the better for our words.
Are they return'd?
   Lorenzo
                       Madam, they are not yet.
But there is come a messenger before
To signify their coming.
   Portia
                       Go in, Nerissa:
Give order to my servants that they take
120 No note at all of our being absent hence—
Nor you, Lorenzo, Jessica nor you.

A tucket sounds

Lorenzo
Your husband is at hand, I hear his trumpet.
We are no telltales, madam; fear you not.
  Portia
This night methinks is but the daylight sick,
125 It looks a little paler; 'tis a day
Such as the day is when the sun is hid.

Enter Bassanio, Antonio, Gratiano, *and their*
followers

  Bassanio
We should hold day with the Antipodes,
If you would walk in absence of the sun.
  Portia
Let me give light, but let me not be light,
130 For a light wife doth make a heavy husband,
And never be Bassanio so for me—
But God sort all! You are welcome home, my lord.
  Bassanio
I thank you, madam. Give welcome to my friend.
This is the man, this is Antonio,
135 To whom I am so infinitely bound.
  Portia
You should in all sense be much bound to him,
For as I hear he was much bound for you.
  Antonio
No more than I am well acquitted of.
  Portia
Sir, you are very welcome to our house.
140 It must appear in other ways than words:
Therefore I scant this breathing courtesy.
  Gratiano
[*To* Nerissa] By yonder moon I swear you do me
    wrong!
In faith, I gave it to the judge's clerk,
Would he were gelt that had it, for my part,
145 Since you do take it, love, so much at heart.
  Portia
A quarrel ho, already! What's the matter?

127–8 *We . . . sun*: if you were to walk at night, it would be daylight here as well as on the other side of the globe ('the Antipodes').
129 *be light*: be faithless.
130 *heavy*: sorrowful.
131 *for me*: because of what I have done.
132 *sort all*: decide everything.

135 *bound*: indebted.

137 *bound*: in chains as a prisoner.

138 *acquitted of*: repaid for (with the love of Bassanio).

141 *scant*: cut short.
    breathing courtesy: verbal politeness.

144 *Would . . . gelt*: I wish he had been castrated.
145 *take . . . heart*: care so much about it.

Gratiano

About a hoop of gold, a paltry ring

That she did give me, whose poesy was

For all the world like cutler's poetry

150 Upon a knife: 'Love me, and leave me not.'

Nerissa

What talk you of the poesy or the value?

You swore to me when I did give it you,

That you would wear it till your hour of death,

And that it should lie with you in your grave.

155 Though not for me, yet for your vehement oaths

You should have been respective and have kept it.

Gave it a judge's clerk! No, God's my judge

The clerk will ne'er wear hair on's face that had it.

Gratiano

He will, and if he live to be a man.

Nerissa

160 Ay, if a woman live to be a man.

Gratiano

Now by this hand, I gave it to a youth,

A kind of boy, a little scrubbed boy

No higher than thyself, the judge's clerk,

A prating boy that begg'd it as a fee;

165 I could not for my heart deny it him.

Portia

You were to blame, I must be plain with you,

To part so slightly with your wife's first gift,

A thing stuck on with oaths upon your finger

And so riveted with faith unto your flesh.

170 I gave my love a ring, and made him swear

Never to part with it, and here he stands.

I dare be sworn for him he would not leave it

Nor pluck it from his finger for the wealth

That the world masters. Now in faith, Gratiano,

175 You give your wife too unkind a cause of grief;

And 'twere to me, I should be mad at it.

Bassanio

[*Aside*] Why, I were best to cut my left hand off

And swear I lost the ring defending it.

Gratiano

My lord Bassanio gave his ring away

---

148 *poesy*: motto engraved inside a ring.

149 *cutler's poetry*: doggerel verse inscribed on a knife-handle.

151 *What*: why.

155 *for me*: for my sake.

158 *wear hair on's face*: grow a beard.

159 *and if*: if ever.

162 *scrubbed*: scrubbèd; stunted.

164 *prating*: chattering.

172 *leave*: part with.

174 *masters*: is master of.

176 *And 'twere to me*: if it had been done to me.

180 Unto the judge that begg'd it, and indeed
Deserv'd it too; and then the boy his clerk

182 *pains*: care.

That took some pains in writing, he begg'd mine,
And neither man nor master would take aught
But the two rings.

> **Portia**
>   What ring gave you, my lord?

185 Not that, I hope, which you receiv'd of me?

> **Bassanio**
> If I could add a lie unto a fault,
> I would deny it; but you see my finger
> Hath not the ring upon it, it is gone.

> **Portia**

189 *void*: empty.

> Even so void is your false heart of truth.

190 By heaven, I will ne'er come in your bed
Until I see the ring.

> **Nerissa**
>   Nor I in yours
> Till I again see mine.

> **Bassanio**
>   Sweet Portia,
> If you did know to whom I gave the ring,
> If you did know for whom I gave the ring,

195 And would conceive for what I gave the ring,
And how unwillingly I left the ring,
When naught would be accepted but the ring,
You would abate the strength of your displeasure.

> **Portia**

199–202 *If . . . ring*: Portia parodies Bassanio's figure of speech (epistrophe).
199 *virtue*: special quality.
201 *contain*: keep.

> If you had known the virtue of the ring,

200 Or half her worthiness that gave the ring,
Or your own honour to contain the ring,
You would not then have parted with the ring.
What man is there so much unreasonable,
If you had pleas'd to have defended it

205 *terms of zeal*: determination.
205–6 *wanted . . . ceremony*: would have been so indelicate to press for something held sacred.

205 With any terms of zeal, wanted the modesty
To urge the thing held as a ceremony?
Nerissa teaches me what to believe:

208 *I'll die for't*: I am ready to die for my belief.

> I'll die for't, but some woman had the ring!

> **Bassanio**
> No by my honour, madam, by my soul

210 *civil doctor*: doctor of civil law.

210 No woman had it, but a civil doctor,

213 *suffer'd*: allowed.
214 *held up*: saved.

217 *beset*: overcome.

219 *besmear*: stain.

220 *blessed*: blessèd.
candles of the night: the stars.

222 *of*: from.

Which did refuse three thousand ducats of me,
And begg'd the ring, the which I did deny him,
And suffer'd him to go displeas'd away,
Even he that had held up the very life
215 Of my dear friend. What should I say, sweet lady?
I was enforc'd to send it after him;
I was beset with shame and courtesy;
My honour would not let ingratitude
So much besmear it. Pardon me, good lady,
220 For by these blessed candles of the night,
Had you been there I think you would have begg'd
The ring of me to give the worthy doctor.

Portia

Let not that doctor e'er come near my house.
Since he hath got the jewel that I lov'd
225 And that which you did swear to keep for me,
I will become as liberal as you;
I'll not deny him anything I have,
No, not my body, nor my husband's bed:
Know him I shall, I am well sure of it.

230 *Lie . . . home*: don't spend a single night away from home.
Argus: A monster of classical mythology who closed only two of his hundred eyes at any one time.
232 *yet mine own*: still intact.

234 *be well advis'd*: take good care.

235 *to mine own protection*: to look after my own honour.

236 *take*: catch.

237 *I'll mar . . . pen*: I'll ruin his equipment.

230 Lie not a night from home. Watch me like Argus.
If you do not, if I be left alone,
Now by mine honour which is yet mine own,
I'll have that doctor for my bedfellow.

Nerissa

And I his clerk; therefore be well advis'd
235 How you do leave me to mine own protection.

Gratiano

Well, do you so. Let not me take him then,
For if I do, I'll mar the young clerk's pen.

Antonio

I am th'unhappy subject of these quarrels.

Portia

Sir, grieve not you; you are welcome notwithstanding.

Bassanio

240 *enforced*: enforcèd.

240 Portia, forgive me this enforced wrong;
And in the hearing of these many friends
I swear to thee, even by thine own fair eyes
Wherein I see myself—

Portia

Mark you but that?

245 *double*: a) two-fold; b) two-faced.
246 *of credit*: that can be believed.

249 *wealth*: well-being, happiness.

251 *miscarried*: been lost.
252 *My . . . forfeit*: at the risk of forfeiting my soul.
253 *advisedly*: knowingly.

254 *surety*: security.

261 *scrubbed*: scrubbèd.
262 *In lieu of*: in return for.

263–4 *mending . . . enough*: repairing good roads unnecessarily in summertime; Gratiano is saying that this situation is ridiculous.
265 *cuckolds*: men whose wives are unfaithful to them.
deserv'd it: i.e. by showing themselves to be unsatisfactory lovers.
266 *grossly*: crudely.
amaz'd: bewildered.

In both my eyes he doubly sees himself:
245 In each eye one. Swear by your double self,
And there's an oath of credit!
Bassanio
                        Nay, but hear me.
Pardon this fault, and by my soul I swear
I nevermore will break an oath with thee.
Antonio
I once did lend my body for his wealth,
250 Which but for him that had your husband's ring
Had quite miscarried. I dare be bound again,
My soul upon the forfeit, that your lord
Will nevermore break faith advisedly.
Portia
Then you shall be his surety. Give him this,
255 And bid him keep it better than the other.
Antonio
Here, Lord Bassanio, swear to keep this ring.
Bassanio
By heaven, it is the same I gave the doctor!
Portia
I had it of him; pardon me, Bassanio,
For by this ring the doctor lay with me.
Nerissa
260 And pardon me, my gentle Gratiano,
For that same scrubbed boy the doctor's clerk,
In lieu of this, last night did lie with me.
Gratiano
Why, this is like the mending of highways
In summer where the ways are fair enough!
265 What, are we cuckolds ere we have deserv'd it?
Portia
Speak not so grossly; you are all amaz'd.
Here is a letter, read it at your leisure;
It comes from Padua, from Bellario.
There you shall find that Portia was the doctor,
270 Nerissa there her clerk. Lorenzo here
Shall witness I set forth as soon as you,
And even but now return'd; I have not yet
Enter'd my house. Antonio, you are welcome;
And I have better news in store for you

275 *soon*: quickly.

279 *chanced*: chancèd.

288 *road*: anchorage.

294 *manna*: the food from heaven that sustained the Israelites starving in the desert (Exodus 16:14–15).
295 *starved*: starvèd.

297 *at full*: in detail.
298 *charge . . . inter'gatories*: interrogate us on oath.

275 Than you expect. Unseal this letter soon;
There you shall find three of your argosies
Are richly come to harbour suddenly.
You shall not know by what strange accident
I chanced on this letter.

Antonio
                                        I am dumb.

Bassanio
280 Were you the doctor and I knew you not?

Gratiano
Were you the clerk that is to make me cuckold?

Nerissa
Ay, but the clerk that never means to do it,
Unless he live until he be a man.

Bassanio
Sweet doctor, you shall be my bedfellow;
285 When I am absent, then lie with my wife.

Antonio
Sweet lady, you have given me life and living;
For here I read for certain that my ships
Are safely come to road.

Portia
                                        How now, Lorenzo?
My clerk hath some good comforts too for you.

Nerissa
290 Ay, and I'll give them him without a fee.
There do I give to you and Jessica
From the rich Jew, a special deed of gift
After his death of all he dies possess'd of.

Lorenzo
Fair ladies, you drop manna in the way
295 Of starved people.

Portia
                                        It is almost morning;
And yet I am sure you are not satisfied
Of these events at full. Let us go in,
And charge us there upon inter'gatories,
And we will answer all things faithfully.

Gratiano
300 Let it be so. The first inter'gatory
That my Nerissa shall be sworn on is:

Whether till the next night she had rather stay,
Or go to bed now, being two hours to day.
But were the day come, I should wish it dark,
305 Till I were couching with the doctor's clerk.
Well, while I live I'll fear no other thing
So sore as keeping safe Nerissa's ring.   [*Exeunt*

305 *couching*: going to bed.
306 *while I live*: as long as I live.
306–7 *I'll . . . ring*: I'll take care of
nothing so much as guarding Nerissa's
ring (and also her honour).

The Merchant of Venice: the Source

The lady, the pound of flesh, and the ring

The most likely source for the main plot in *The Merchant of Venice* seems to have been one of the stories in *Il Pecorone* (= 'the big sheep', or dunce), a collection of tales by Ser Giovanni of Florence, which was published at Milan in 1558. No English version has ever been found – so we must assume that Shakespeare read the original in Italian.

Ansaldo, a wealthy merchant of Venice, financed his godson Giannetto in his attempts to win the Lady of Belmont. This Lady was a rich widow who had agreed to marry the first man who succeeded in making love to her – but she had imposed the condition that all unsuccessful lovers must forfeit everything they possessed. Giannetto twice attempted this task; and both times he failed – because he was given drugged wine to make him fall asleep before the lady came to bed. Because he was ashamed of his failures, he told Ansaldo that he had twice been shipwrecked. Determined to make a third attempt, he begged Ansaldo for more money. This time Ansaldo was forced to borrow ten thousand ducats from a Jew to enable him to equip yet another ship for Giannetto. The Jew made the condition that if the loan were not repaid upon St John's Day, the merchant would forfeit a pound of his own flesh.

Giannetto (warned by a maid not to drink the drugged wine) succeeded in making love to the lady; he married her, and was proclaimed sovereign of all that she possessed. He forgot about Ansaldo's bargain with the Jew until St John's Day arrived, and then he told his wife the whole story. The Lady sent Giannetto to Venice with enough money to repay the Jew; and she herself followed him, disguised as a lawyer.

The Jew refused to accept Giannetto's money, because he wanted to say that he had killed the greatest of all the Christian merchants. The 'lawyer' claimed that she could settle all disputes, and she heard the Jew's case against Ansaldo, with Giannetto's offer to repay the debt. She advised the Jew to take the ten thousand ducats, but he persisted in refusing. She then told him to take the pound of flesh – but, at the last moment, she warned him that if he took more than an exact pound, or shed one drop of blood, he would be executed. The Jew then asked for the money instead of the flesh. When this was refused, he tore up the bond.

Giannetto offered the ducats as a fee to the 'lawyer', but she demanded to be given his ring. He then returned to Belmont, taking Ansaldo with him. The Lady accused Giannetto of giving the ring to one of his former mistresses. He wept, but finally the Lady explained everything – and Ansaldo married the maid who had warned Giannetto about the drugged wine.

The caskets   The casket story may have been suggested by the account in History 32 of *Gesta Romanorum*, translated by R. Robinson in 1595, where the heroine was told to make a choice between three 'vessels' in order to win a husband.

'The first [vessel] was made of pure gold, well-beset with precious stones without, and within full of dead men's bones; and thereupon was engraved this poesy: *Whoso chooseth me shall find that he deserveth*. The second vessel was made of fine silver, filled with earth and worms; and the superscription was thus: *Whoso chooseth me shall find that his nature desireth*. The third vessel was made of lead, full within of precious stones; and thereupon was ensculped this poesy: *Whoso chooseth me, shall find that God hath disposed for him*.'

The Jew and his daughter   A contemporary play, *The Jew of Malta* (c. 1589) by Christopher Marlowe, gave Shakespeare some inspiration for the character of Shylock. Marlowe's Jew, Barabas, is determined to be revenged on the Christians who persecute him; and he too has a daughter who loves a Christian. Shylock's lament – 'My daughter! O my ducats! O my daughter!' (Act 2, Scene 8, line 15) – seems to be modelled on Barabas's cry: 'Oh my girl! My gold, my fortune . . . Oh girl! Oh gold! Oh beauty! Oh my bliss!' (*The Jew of Malta*, Act 2, Scene 2, lines 47–54).

Background

England in 1599

When Shakespeare was writing *The Merchant of Venice*, many people still believed that the sun went round the earth. They were taught that this was the way God had ordered things, and that – in England – God had founded a Church and appointed a Monarchy so that the land and people could be well governed.

'The past is a foreign country; they do things differently there.'

L. P. Hartley

Government   For most of Shakespeare's life, the reigning monarch of England was Queen Elizabeth I. With her counsellors and ministers, she governed the nation from London, although fewer than half a million people out of a total population of six million lived in the capital city. In the rest of the country, law and order were maintained by the land-owners and enforced by their deputies. The average man had no vote, and women had no rights at all.

Religion   At this time, England was a Christian country. All children were baptized, soon after they were born, into the Church of England; they were taught the essentials of the Christian faith, and instructed in their duty to God and to humankind. Marriages and funerals were conducted only by the licensed clergy and according to the Church's rites and ceremonies. Attending divine service was compulsory; absences (without a good medical reason) could be punished by fines. By such means, the authorities were able to keep some control over the population – recording births, marriages, and deaths; being alert to anyone who refused to accept standard religious practices, who could be politically dangerous; and ensuring that people received the approved teachings through the official 'Homilies' which were regularly preached in all parish churches.

Elizabeth I's father, Henry VIII, had broken away from the Church of Rome, and from that time all people in England were able to hear the church services *in their own language* rather than in Latin. The Book of Common Prayer was used in every church, and an English translation of the Bible was read aloud in public. The Christian religion had never been so well taught before!

Education
School education reinforced the Church's teaching. From the age of four, boys might attend the 'petty school' (its name came from the French '*petite école*') to learn reading and writing along with a few prayers; some schools also included work with numbers. At the age of seven, the boy was ready for the grammar school (if his father was willing and able to pay the fees).

Grammar schools taught Latin grammar, translation work and the study of Roman authors, paying attention as much to style as to content. The art of fine writing was therefore important from early youth. A very few students went on to university; these were either clever boys who won scholarships, or else the sons of rich noblemen. Girls stayed at home, and learned domestic and social skills – cooking, sewing, perhaps even music. The lucky ones might learn to read and write.

Language
At the start of the sixteenth century the English had a very poor opinion of their own language: there was little serious writing in English, and hardly any literature. Latin was the language of international scholarship, and the eloquent style of the Romans was much admired. Many translations from Latin were made, and in this way writers increased the vocabulary of English and made its grammar more flexible. French, Italian, and Spanish works were also translated and, for the first time, there were English versions of the Bible. By the end of the century, English was a language to be proud of: it was rich in vocabulary, capable of infinite variety and subtlety, and ready for all kinds of word-play – especially *puns*, for which Elizabethan English is renowned.

Drama
The great art-form of the Elizabethan and Jacobean age was drama. The Elizabethans inherited a tradition of play-acting from the Middle Ages, and they reinforced this by reading and translating the Roman playwrights. At the beginning of the sixteenth century plays were performed by groups of actors. These were all-male companies (boys acted the female roles) who travelled from town to town, setting up their stages in open places (such as inn-yards) or,

with the permission of the owner, in the hall of some noble house. The touring companies continued outside London into the seventeenth century; but in London, in 1576, a new building was erected for the performance of plays. This was the Theatre, the first purpose-built playhouse in England. Other playhouses followed, including the Globe, where most of Shakespeare's plays were performed, and English drama reached new heights.

There were people who disapproved, of course. The theatres, which brought large crowds together, could encourage the spread of disease – and dangerous ideas. During the summer, when the plague was at its worst, the playhouses were closed. A constant censorship was imposed, more or less severe at different times. The Puritans, a religious and political faction who wanted to impose strict rules of behaviour, tried to close down the theatres. However, partly because the royal family favoured drama, and partly because the buildings were outside the city limits, they did not succeed until 1642.

Theatre   From contemporary comments and sketches – most particularly a drawing by a Dutch visitor, Johannes de Witt – it is possible to form some idea of the typical Elizabethan playhouse for which most of Shakespeare's plays were written. Hexagonal (six-sided) in shape, it

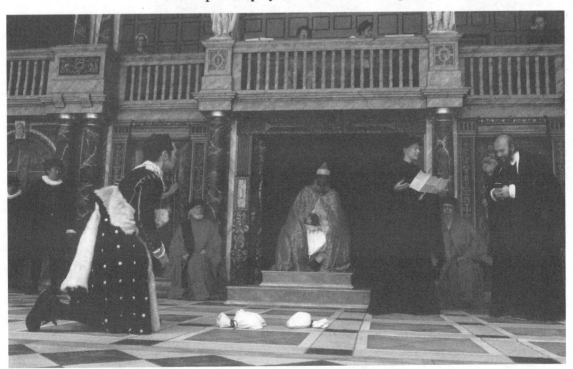

had three roofed galleries encircling an open courtyard. The plain, high stage projected into the yard, where it was surrounded by the audience of standing 'groundlings'. At the back were two doors for the actors' entrances and exits; and above these doors was a balcony – useful for a musicians' gallery or for the acting of scenes '*above*'. Over the stage was a thatched roof, supported on two pillars, forming a canopy – which seems to have been painted with the sun, moon, and stars for the 'heavens'.

Underneath was space (concealed by curtains) which could be used by characters ascending and descending through a trap-door in the stage. Costumes and properties were kept backstage in the 'tiring house'. The actors used the most luxurious costumes they could find, often clothes given to them by rich patrons. Stage properties were important for showing where a scene was set, but the dramatist's own words were needed to explain the time of day, since all performances took place in the early afternoon.

A replica of Shakespeare's own theatre, the Globe, has been built in London, and stands in Southwark, almost exactly on the Bankside site of the original.

William Shakespeare, 1564–1616

Elizabeth I was Queen of England when Shakespeare was born in 1564. He was the son of a tradesman who made and sold gloves in the small town of Stratford-upon-Avon, and he was educated at the grammar school in that town. Shakespeare did not go to university when he left school, but worked, perhaps, in his father's business. When he was eighteen he married Anne Hathaway, who became the mother of his daughter, Susanna, in 1583, and of twins in 1585.

There is nothing exciting, or even unusual, in this story; and from 1585 until 1592 there are no documents that can tell us anything at all about Shakespeare. But we have learned that in 1592 he was known in London, and that he had become both an actor and a playwright.

We do not know when Shakespeare wrote his first play, and we are not sure of the order in which he wrote his works. If you look on page 109 at the list of his writings and their approximate dates, you will see he started by writing plays on subjects taken from the history of England. No doubt this was partly because he was patriotic and interested in English history, but he was also a very shrewd businessman. He could see that the theatre audiences enjoyed being shown their own history, and it was certain that he would make a profit from this kind of drama.

He also wrote comedies, with romantic love-stories of young people who fall in love with one another, and at the end of the play marry and live happily ever after.

At the end of the sixteenth century Shakespeare wrote some melancholy, bitter, and tragic plays. This change may have been caused by some sadness in the writer's life (his only son died in 1596). Shakespeare, however, was not the only writer whose works at this time were very serious. The whole of England was facing a crisis. Queen Elizabeth I was growing old. She was greatly loved, and the people were sad to think she must soon die; they were also afraid, because the queen had never married, and so there was no child to succeed her.

When James I, Elizabeth's Scottish cousin, came to the throne in 1603, Shakespeare continued to write serious drama – the great tragedies and the plays based on Roman history (such as *Julius Caesar*) for which he is most famous. Finally, before he retired from the theatre, he wrote another set of comedies. These all have the same theme: they tell of happiness which is lost, and then found again.

Shakespeare returned from London to Stratford, his home town. He was rich and successful, and he owned one of the biggest houses in the town. He died in 1616.

Shakespeare also wrote two long poems, and a collection of sonnets. The sonnets describe two love affairs, but we do not know who the lovers were – or whether they existed only in Shakespeare's imagination. Although there are many public documents concerned with his career as a writer and a businessman, Shakespeare has hidden his personal life from us. A nineteenth-century poet, Matthew Arnold, addressed Shakespeare in a poem, and wrote 'We ask and ask – Thou smilest, and art still'.

There is not even a portrait of the world's greatest dramatist that we can be sure is really of Shakespeare, and painted by someone who had seen him.

Approximate Dates of Composition of Shakespeare's Works

Period	Comedies	History plays	Tragedies	Poems
I before 1594	Comedy of Errors Taming of the Shrew Two Gentlemen of Verona Love's Labour's Lost	Henry VI, part 1 Henry VI, part 2 Henry VI, part 3 Richard III	Titus Andronicus	Venus and Adonis Rape of Lucrece
II 1594 – 1599	Midsummer Night's Dream Merchant of Venice Merry Wives of Windsor Much Ado About Nothing As You Like It	Richard II King John Henry IV, part 1 Henry IV, part 2 Henry V	Romeo and Juliet	Sonnets
III 1599 – 1608	Twelfth Night Troilus and Cressida Measure for Measure All's Well That Ends Well Pericles		Julius Caesar Hamlet Othello Timon of Athens King Lear Macbeth Antony and Cleopatra Coriolanus	
IV 1608 – 1613	Cymbeline The Winter's Tale The Tempest	Henry VIII		

Shakespeare's Globe, Southwark, London, England. Photograph by Richard Kalina.

Exploring *The Merchant of Venice* in the Classroom

Exotic characters and settings as well as electrifying plots and hotly debated themes make *The Merchant of Venice* an excellent choice for study.

This section suggests a range of approaches in the classroom, to help bring the text to life and to engender both enjoyment and understanding of the play.

Ways into the Play

Students may feel an antipathy towards the study of Shakespeare. The imaginative and enthusiastic teacher, with the help of this edition of the play, will soon break this down!

What's in a name?

The names of Shakespeare's characters are often familiar, even without knowledge of the plays themselves. Have any of the students heard the name Shylock? Discuss what sort of character he might be. Give students time to consider the characters behind these names: Antonio, Portia, Lancelot Gobbo. They can compare their ideas with the actual characters as the plays unfolds.

Pictures

Every picture tells a story, so ask your students to look at the picture on page vii and to guess who the characters are and what is happening. Once they are more familiar with the play, ask them to hazard a guess at the exact moment in the play that is depicted.

Navigating the play

Your students may need some help and practice at finding their way around a Shakespeare play. After explaining the division into acts, scenes and lines, challenge them to look up some references as quickly as possible. Refer them to some of the famous lines and those which might lead on to further discussion of the plot. Below are some suggestions:

Act 2, Scene 7, line 65   (*All that glisters is not gold*)
Act 3, Scene 1, line 57   (*If you prick us, do we not bleed?*)
Act 4, Scene 1, line 182   (*The quality of mercy is not strain'd*)

Improvisation

Working on these improvisations may help students access some of the ideas behind the drama.

a) Improvise a scene between two friends – A and B. B is asking A for a loan. B feels embarrassed asking for help, but the loan is for something important and so s/he tries really hard to persuade A. How does A react? Does B get the loan? Are they still friends?

b) Repeat the above improvisation, only this time A is not a friend. In fact B has been rude and horrible to A in the past. How will B try to persuade A? Does B receive the loan?

c) Devise a new TV game show called *Gamble*. In order to win brilliant prizes, participants need to be prepared to gamble things they already have. What would they be prepared to gamble (e.g. their CD collection, all their computer games, pocket money for a year)? Three people play, but only one can win. Students will need to devise the game, and improvise the show.

Setting the Scene

Shylock the Jew

The portrayal of Jews, and in particular Shylock, makes this play controversial. Despite the title of the play, Shylock is the character that makes this play so colourful, and his character is riddled with the stereotypes and prejudices of the Elizabethan Age. Students will need to know that Jews were vilified and expelled from many countries. In those places where they were allowed to remain, often the only occupation open to them was money lending, and in consequence they were even more unpopular.

It has been suggested that because the treatment of Shylock is so grotesque, the play should no longer be performed. But in many ways this is what makes the play so fruitful for study. Use the spotlight of drama to examine prejudices then and now. You can ask how sympathetic Shakespeare is to Shylock. Is the ghastly treatment of Shylock a product of the playwright's own views or Elizabethan society?

Belmont and Venice

There are two main settings for the play:

● Venice: the thriving hub of international trade, inhabited by those involved in the cut and thrust of business and commerce;

● Belmont: an imaginary setting, a civilized and romantic place, home to the gracious Portia.

If you can, show students some pictures of Venice, showing the canals, architecture, markets, etc. Challenge students to design two different sets for Act 1, Scenes 1 and 2. Their designs should aim to illustrate the contrast between the two worlds of the play.

Riddles

The caskets which must be chosen by Portia's suitors bear the following labels:

Gold: *Who chooseth me, shall gain what many men desire.*
Silver: *Who chooseth me, shall get as much as he deserves.*
Lead: *Who chooseth me, must give and hazard all he hath.*

Students can speculate on the possible meanings behind these labels, and decide which casket holds promise and which threatens.

Keeping Track of the Action

It's important to give students opportunities to 'digest' and reflect upon their reading, so that they may take ownership of the play.

Reading journal

As you read through the play, help students to trace and understand the main plot and sub-plots by asking them to keep a journal in which they record what happens. They can also record their reactions and thoughts about the action and the characters. Help them to keep their comments focused by giving them specific questions to answer.

Four stories in one

Shakespeare blends four stories in *The Merchant of Venice.*

The main plot:

● the fortunes of Antonio, Shylock and the pound of flesh.

Three sub-plots:

● Portia and her suitors

● the elopement of Jessica

● the lovers' rings.

Ask the students to use a flowchart to trace each strand of the story. They can look for the links between the stories, as well as analysing how much time Shakespeare devotes to each plot and the relative importance of each part of the overall plot.

Question wall

There are many things that are difficult or puzzling when studying Shakespeare, but asking questions publicly can be daunting for many students. Put blank sticky notes on their desks, and encourage them to write questions or make observations on the notes as the lesson progresses. The notes can then be stuck on a dedicated section of wall in the classroom. At the end of the session, leave enough time to refer to their points and queries. Answer the questions yourself, throw them open to discussion, or promise to do some research if you don't know the answer!

Mini saga

Once the class has read/seen the play, challenge students to retell the story of *The Merchant of Venice* in their own words. Their version should be exactly 50 words long – no more, no less. They might tell the whole story or retell one of the sub-plots. An alternative (possibly extension) activity is to retell the story in verse. See *Shakespeare in a Nutshell: A Rhyming Guide to All the Plays* (listed in Further Reading) for inspiration on Shakespeare in rhyme.

Characters

Students of all ages need to come to an understanding of the characters: their motivations, their relationships, and their development.

Fluctuating fortunes

The fortunes of Antonio and Shylock alternately wax and wane. Ask students to chart the fortunes of both characters, with a simple line graph for each one. With a scale of numbers – say from 1 to 10 – on one axis, and key moments from the play on the other, ask them to plot the fortunes of both.

Suitable points in the play are:

Act 1, Scene 3	Antonio asks Shylock for a loan.
Act 2, Scene 8	Solanio and Salarino gossip about both men.
Act 3, Scene 1	Shylock exchanges views with Solanio and Salarino.
Act 3, Scene 3	Antonio is arrested.
Act 4, Scene 1 (start)	The court seeks the mercy of Shylock.
Act 4, Scene 1 (end)	Shylock is crushed.

The completed graphs can be compared and the fortunes of both characters contrasted.

Thought tracking

This is an excellent way of encouraging students to explore the inner thoughts and motivations of a character. Select a scene where the character's words have hidden meaning, irony or layers of meaning. Ask students to consider and write down the thoughts behind the character's words. Suitable scenes include:

Act 1, Scene 3, lines 133–end *(Antonio and Shylock agree to the bond.)*
Act 2, Scene 7, lines 1–12   *(Portia leads Morocco to the caskets.)*
Act 4, Scene 1, lines 406–end *(The disguised Portia asks Bassanio for a ring.)*

A different perspective

Allowing your students the opportunity to think, write and talk as one of the characters gives them a new and illuminating perspective on the character(s). Here are some possible tasks:

a) Act 2, Scene 6: Jessica leaves a note to her father, explaining her decision to run away and take his wealth.
b) Act 3, Scene 2: On his arrival at Belmont, Bassanio makes a video diary disclosing his hopes and fears.
c) Act 4, Scene 1: A television interview with Shylock prior to the trial, asking him about his intentions.

Shylock – sinned against or sinner?

One of the main decisions a modern director must make is how to portray Shylock – an immoral monster or the bruised product of a deeply prejudiced society. The answer, of course, is that he is probably somewhere between the two.

Look for images of Shylock on the Internet (e.g. through an image search on Google). Give a set of images to the students and ask them to discuss the types of person portrayed.

Set up a debate within your class with one half looking for evidence of the stereotypical, money-grabbing character, and the other half looking for evidence of the wronged and abused Shylock. Debate what type of character he is and how they think Shakespeare intended him to be played. How would they depict him in a modern production?

Themes

Front page

There are many themes and key ideas in the play, for example, justice, friendship, religion, money and love. Ask students to produce a newspaper front page which reflects and explores some of the themes throughout the play. Their news stories might cover aspects such as Portia's suitors, the bond and the fate of Antonio's ships.

Fathers and daughters

'…so is the will of a living daughter curbed by the will of a dead father.' Portia's father controls his daughter even after his death, with the lottery of caskets he has set up. Jessica is also under the firm control of her father. The only way she can escape from his control is to renounce him completely and elope. Both women will come under the control of their husbands.

Use the play to look for evidence of the position of women in Shakespearean times, and discuss how things have changed. Ask for two volunteers to take on the roles of Portia and Jessica, and 'hot seat' both characters. Encourage the chosen students to take on an authentic sixteenth-century role and allow the rest of the class to ask them about their positions, their feelings, and hopes for the future.

The two women deal very differently with their situations. Ask the students which one they admire most and why.

Judge a book by its cover

Ask students to design a new cover for this book or for a programme for a performance of the play. The cover should reveal something of the themes of the play as well as giving essential information.

Shakespeare's Language

The language of persuasion

There are several speeches that seek to persuade, the most notable of which must be Portia's lines in Act 4, Scene 1, lines 182ff ('The quality of mercy is not strain'd'). Ask the class to read the speech, with each student reading up to a punctuation mark before the next student takes over.

Ask students to analyse how the speech is persuasive. They can look at the structure of the speech: the build-up from looking at the simple nature of mercy, to mercy in the hands of kings, right up to the mercy of God. Finally there is a direct plea to Shylock for mercy.

Students can also look for ideas and words that are repeated; analogies and associations (e.g. to kings and God); religious references; allusions to power and greatness; and the use of pronouns (e.g. 'us') to establish common ground. Discuss how each of the techniques works.

The language of hate

In Act 1, Scene 3, lines 101–24, Shylock famously relates how he has been abused and insulted. Ask the class to read the speech, with each student reading out one line before moving on to the next student. Ask them to read the speech again, but this time reading only one word from the line – the word that they consider to be the most important or significant. Discuss their choices, then ask them to look at the words and ideas that are repeated (e.g. dog, spit). What is the effect of the words on the reader, and what does this speech reveal about Shylock and Antonio?

The language of love

The words of the lovers are courtly and formalized. Examine the speech where Bassanio opens the lead casket to find Portia's picture (Act 3, Scene 2, lines 114–30). Have some fun with a dramatic reading of this section of the speech by putting students into pairs – one of them reading the lines and the other miming the actions. The reader should aim for an exaggerated and melodramatic presentation which emphasizes the overstated images and tone of the passage.

After students have read the scroll, give them a cloze version of lines 139–48, with some of the end rhymes removed. This will enable them to focus on the rhyming couplets and how rhyme can draw attention to words and ideas.

Exploring with Drama

Book the hall or push back the desks, because the best way to study a great play is through drama. Students of all ages will benefit from a dramatic encounter with *The Merchant of Venice*. They will enjoy the opportunity to act out a scene or two, or to explore the situations through improvisation, for example, putting a character in the 'hot seat' for questioning by others.

Tableaux

Ask your students to create a tableau or freeze-frame involving all the characters in the play. The characters should be grouped together according to their relationships in the play, and their positions should say something about their interactions and status within the scene/play. Bring the tableau briefly to life by having each person saying something in character.

Alternatively, put the students into groups. Each group should create a tableau of one 'family' of characters or one moment in the play. One student from each group should be a 'sculptor' and mould the rest of the group into position.

The trial

Before they read or watch the trial scene from the play, give students a précis of the situation and ask them to prepare an improvisation of the trial. Divide up the parts among the class: jury; Shylock and his prosecution team; Antonio and his defence team; a judge; television reporters. Give them time to prepare their speeches and questions.

Their improvisation will not feature the device of a disguised Portia, of course, but it will enable students to establish and engage with the two sides of the case. It will be also be interesting to see how the judge sums up the case, whom the jury side with, and how the press report the event in a one-minute report 'to camera' (to the class). They can go on to compare their trial with Shakespeare's version.

The director

This is a play of famous speeches. Choose one speech (e.g. Act 1, Scene 3, lines 101–32) and put students into small groups, according to how many people are in the scene. They will also require one student to act as director. The director must then direct the other student(s) to give an action reading of the scene, so they can use their scripts but must act out the lines. Encourage the director to annotate a copy of the script, detailing his or her decisions. View and explore the different interpretations and decisions that different groups make.

Writing about *The Merchant of Venice*

If your students have to write about *The Merchant of Venice* for coursework or for examinations, you may wish to give them this general guidance.

- Read the question or task carefully, highlight the key words and answer all parts of the question.
- Planning is essential. Plan what will be in each paragraph. You can change your plan if necessary.
- Avoid retelling the story.
- *The Merchant of Venice* is a play – so consider the impact or effect on the audience.
- Use the Point, Evidence, Explanation (PEE) structure to explain points.
- Adding Evaluation (PEEE!) will gain you higher marks.
- Keep quotations short and relevant.
- Avoid referring to a film version of the play, unless this is part of your task.

Further Reading and Resources

General

Fantasia, Louis, *Instant Shakespeare: A Practical Guide for Actors, Directors and Teachers* (A & C Black, 2002).

Greer, Germaine, *Shakespeare: A Very Short Introduction* (Oxford, 2002).

Hall, Peter, *Shakespeare's Advice to the Players* (Oberon Books, 2003).

Holden, Anthony, *Shakespeare: His Life and Work* (Abacus, 2002).

Kneen, Judith, *Teaching Shakespeare from Transition to Test* (Oxford University Press, 2004).

McConnell, Louise, *Exit, Pursued by a Bear – Shakespeare's Characters, Plays, Poems, History and Stagecraft* (Bloomsbury, 2003).

McLeish, Kenneth, and Unwin, Stephen, *A Pocket Guide to Shakespeare's Plays* (Faber and Faber, 1998).

Muirden, James, *Shakespeare in a Nutshell: A Rhyming Guide to All the Plays* (Constable, 2004).

Wood, Michael, *In Search of Shakespeare* (BBC, 2003).

Children's/Students' Books

Deary, Terry, *Top Ten Shakespeare Stories* (Scholastic, 1998).

Ganeri, Anita, *What They Don't Tell You About Shakespeare* (Hodder, 1996).

Garfield, Leon, *Shakespeare Stories* (Puffin, 1997).

Lamb, Charles and Mary, *Tales from Shakespeare* (Puffin, 1987).

Williams, Marcia, *Bravo, Mr William Shakespeare!* (Walker, 2001).

Websites

The *Complete Works of Shakespeare*
http://the-tech.mit.edu/Shakespeare/

Elizabethan pronunciation
Including information on insults.
http://www.renfaire.com/Language/index.html

Encyclopaedia Britannica – Shakespeare and the Globe: Then and Now
Information about the Globe and the theatre in Shakespeare's times.
http://search.eb.com/shakespeare/index2.html

The Royal Shakespeare Company website
As well as information on the theatre company, there are resources on the plays and the life and times of Shakespeare.
http://www.rsc.org.uk/home/index.asp

The Shakespeare Birthplace Trust
Information on his works, life and times.
http://www.shakespeare.org.uk/homepage

Shakespeare's Globe
Information on the Globe Theatre, London.
http://www.shakespeares-globe.org/

Shakespeare Illustrated
An excellent source of paintings and pictures based on Shakespeare's plays.
http://www.emory.edu/ENGLISH/classes/Shakespeare_Illustrated/Shakespeare.html

Spark Notes: The Merchant of Venice
An online study guide.
http://www.sparknotes.com/shakespeare/merchant/

Mr William Shakespeare and the Internet
A comprehensive guide to Shakespeare resources on the Internet.
http://shakespeare.palomar.edu/

Film, Video and DVD
The Merchant of Venice
Directed by Michael Radford (2004)
Starring Al Pacino, Lynn Collins, Jeremy Irons

The Merchant of Venice
Directed by Trevor Nunn (2000)
Starring Henry Goodman, Derbhle Crotty, David Bamber

Channel 4 *Middle English: The Merchant of Venice*
Starring Bob Peck and Haydn Gwynne (1996)

BBC *Shakespeare – The Merchant of Venice*
Starring Warren Mitchell (1978)